IGNITE YOUR PERFORMANCE & FUEL YOUR SUCCESS

LEADERSHIP IS FOR EVERYONE

20 LEADERSHIP SECRETS FOR EXCEPTIONAL OUTCOMES AND FULFILLMENT AT WORK

VINAY NADIG

ISBN-13: 978-1492291299

Cover and interior layout design by Steven Plummer

Product or brand names used in this book may be trade names or trademarks. Where we believe that there may be proprietary claims to such trade names or trademarks, the name has been used with an initial cap or it has been capitalized in the style used by the name claimant. Regardless of the capitalization used, all such names have been used in an editorial manner without any intent to convey endorsement of or other affiliation with the name claimant. The author does not intend to express any judgement as to the validity or legal status of any such proprietary claim.

This publication is designed to provide accurate and authoritative information in regard to the subject matter covered. It is sold with the understanding that the author is not engaged in rendering legal, accounting, or other professional service. If legal advice or other expert assistance is required, the services of a competent professional person should be sought.

– From a declaration of principles jointly adopted by a Committee of the American Bar Association and a Committee of Publishers.

This book is dedicated to my loving and patient family – my wife Deena, my son Mihir and my daughter Lahar – whose long-suffering endurance of my moods and "writer's blocks" sustained me through this project.

ADVANCE PRAISE FOR
LEADERSHIP IS FOR EVERYONE

In *Leadership IS for Everyone*, Vinay lays out a vision to achieve exceptional performance and achieve fulfillment at work. His core tenets of "doing things" rather than "being somebody", of sustainable behaviors rather than a belief in hierarchy and title hit the mark in today's workplace. Using a practical workbook-like approach, Vinay leads you through the process of establishing yourself as a leader and then launching into the highest levels of leadership where you focus not just on yourself, but in transforming others. If you are looking to take your performance to the next level and achieve not just your goals but true fulfillment, then reading and using the 20 leadership secrets he shares in this book will prove invaluable.

– MARSHALL GOLDSMITH – THE THINKERS50 AWARD WINNER (SPONSORED BY HARVARD BUSINESS REVIEW) FOR MOST-INFLUENTIAL LEADERSHIP THINKER IN THE WORLD & 2 MILLION-SELLING AUTHOR OF THE NEW YORK TIMES BESTSELLERS, *MOJO* AND *WHAT GOT YOU HERE WON'T GET YOU THERE*

Too often, today's business culture rewards leaders for "being" great rather than "doing" great. By tapping into his extensive personal and consulting experience, Vinay corrects this misconception, makes a compelling case for action - skills, accomplishments, credibility and relationships - as the basis of leadership excellence, and provides a roadmap for executives to follow to achieve their career potential.

– MR RANGASWAMI, FOUNDER INDIASPORA, SAND HILL GROUP AND FEATURED IN FORBES MIDAS 100 LIST OF MOST SUCCESSFUL INVESTORS

Leadership, which occurs at every level of an organization, is first about acquiring the skills, then executing, continuing to learn, adapt and fine tune. *Leadership IS for Everyone* is a practical toolkit to help you do exactly that. It offers pragmatic, step by step keys to success.

– CASS WHEELER, RETIRED CEO, AMERICAN HEART ASSOCIATION

In my many years of experience as a public company CEO and as a youth hockey coach I've always just known in my gut that there was a huge value when you could get your staff or players to think "TEAM" vs. "I". Vinay in his book *Leadership IS for Everyone* captures the essence of TEAM and puts it forward to his readers in a manner that is quick and clear to comprehend and with a concise plan that is ready for execution. This is a "must-read" business masterpiece that will have you ready to drive beneficial and highly impactful cultural change in your organization's leadership style and effectiveness in quick fashion.

– MARK C. LAYTON, COO OF VIDEO PLUS, INC. , FOUNDER & FORMER CEO
OF PFSWEB, INC.

Reading and acting on the advice in *Leadership IS for Everyone* will give you much of what you need to be successful in your career. It is filled with practical advice, assessments and recommendations on what it takes to be an admired, successful and respected leader. I found the assessments to be most useful in calibrating where a leader needs to adjust actions and behaviors to take them to a level of extraordinary performance. The focus on values makes this a book not only to read but to put into action in every aspect of business and personal relationships.

– JOHN PAUL, PARTNER, ASSOCIATION WORKS

Vinay has crafted an egalitarian vision of leadership. A system of behaviors that will allow anyone to become a leader, regardless of their title or position. Vinay's concept of leadership as action and not a state of being is spot on and truly empowering. The 20 leadership secrets are applicable not just in business but in all facets of life whether as a parent, spouse, coach etc. This book has inspired me to review my core leadership principles. I wish I (and some of my bosses) could have read this book 25 years ago. This is the best book I've read since the 7 habits.

– DANIEL BANDI, CHIEF INVESTMENT OFFICER, INTEGRITY ASSET
MANAGEMENT

This book is an excellent roadmap to guide individuals to find their "inner leader". It takes you from a range of different stages from reflection, assessment, visioning and action. Following this book will allow you to ascend to the next level.

– HARRY LaROSILIERE, MAYOR – CITY OF PLANO, TX

PREFACE

Until now, leadership has always been viewed as the purview of a select few – it seems to be more about the "what" these leaders want their subjects to do, rather than the "how-to." More often than not, in my decades of experience, leaders are programmed to deliver the "rah rah" speeches, but rarely provide a framework for exceptional performance to those they lead.

Blessing White's *Employee Engagement Report 2011* found that fewer than 1 in 3 employees worldwide (31%) are engaged. Nearly 1 in 5 (17%) are actually disengaged. The report also illustrates that more employees are looking outside of their organizations for opportunities in 2011 than were in 2008. Amongst other reasons, this state of affairs is a failure of leadership – both by the leaders who are in positions of power, and by those who need to perform daily.

With the principles and practices provided in this book, readers will be able to (a) accept the fact that engagement and fulfillment in the workplace is everyone's duty; (b) identify where they fall in the exceptional leader's continuum;

(c) embrace the daily behaviors that are essential to leadership; (d) practice daily leadership behavior; (e) measure their progress and (f) begin to perform at an exceptional level.

Globalization, the world financial crisis, outsourcing, short-term management approaches, and social media have all been charged with crimes against productivity and performance! Whatever the cause, this much is clear: the characteristics of business performance are changing rapidly. No longer can people depend on lifelong employment, the stepladder of promotions and assured assistance from employers for health and retirement and benefits. People at all levels in business are required to constantly deliver value, and continue to innovate in both their personal roles as well as influence the outcomes of their teams. The old ways of working definitely won't cut it, and a recipe for daily leadership behavior is not exactly forthcoming.

However, human nature has not changed. The human need to engage and find fulfillment, the need for peer recognition, rewards and onward progress, the achievement of collective goals greater than individual goals, have not diminished. They are constants, and because they are constants, daily leadership behavior at all levels remains at the heart of driving people toward exceptional performance.

What does this mean to employees, managers and entrepreneurs? A unique opportunity to differentiate, to find relevance in this turbulent world, because companies that employ these individuals will, on a multitude of dimensions, outperform their competitors. And that, ultimately, makes it a worthwhile business objective to support daily leadership behavior.

TABLE OF CONTENTS

WHAT'S THE MAIN IDEA?

High-performing leaders who find fulfillment at work got rid of the notion that "leadership is not for everyone" a long time ago– they truly believe that leadership *is* for everyone. They also firmly believe that leadership has to start from inside – that is, from within ourselves – and the way we show it, use it, achieve benefits out of it – is through others. They understand that we can't serve others if we don't lead from within.

INTRODUCTION

*"It ought to be made possible for everyone to earn
his living by doing work that is of intrinsic value and
that is felt to be such by the worker himself."*
ARNOLD J. TOYNBEE

In close to 25 years of working with people in business, university and sports, I have had the privilege of working with outstanding leaders doing exceptional work. And the vast majority of this time, I have worked with and for individuals who show all the signs of outward success, but are plagued by a sense of unfulfilled destiny. I find that these individuals struggle with their careers, give up on the shiny bright-eyed enthusiasm that brought them to the workplace, and generally muddle through their work lives in mediocrity. The furious pace of global economic change adds significant pressure to this situation and people are left with a feeling of what could have been vs. what can and should be. I have watched and helped people who shared their frustrations, which may reverberate with you:

I started my work life after a tough 4 years of mechanical engineering school. I realize that I am fairly new, but I find that I have no direction in my job, am not able to really understand what I am supposed to do at my work. Even if given certain job goals, I am not really educated on how to achieve them. I don't understand how this can become a career where I can aspire to lead people and accomplish great things.

I think I am a good manager. I give proper direction to my staff and then expect them to take responsibility for their actions. But the moment I turn my back, I feel like I have a group of school kids on my hands – I have to "mother" them back to their tasks. I am frustrated because I know I cannot grow in my job if I have to shepherd my team like this.

I can't stand my boss. But I cannot just up and leave, because the economy is so bad. She micromanages every detail of my job and I feel like I have no freedom whatsoever. I feel like I have the skills to do the job right, but don't have the freedom to execute my tasks. I am frustrated and don't know how to break the shackles of this job.

I have been here for 10 years and now I feel like I have plateaued. When I started, I had some idea about where I wanted to go, but now I feel like I am just trundling along. I am ashamed to say that my work output, while okay – is probably below the best quality that I can produce. I can't believe that I am saying this, but I feel that I get through the day by doing the bare minimum on most days.

I know I have the capability to lead others, but I just don't know how to convince my manager that I should be given charge of a team. I have shown that I can complete my tasks on time and have even saved the company some money during *my last project. It's almost as if they expect me to go above and beyond each time with no possible reward for my efforts.*

I have worked hard, and through a series of promotions have arrived at where I am today. But, I feel stuck now. I feel that my boss doesn't really understand my strengths, and that he doesn't really have a plan for my career. It is always how much more I can do for the company, never about how to fulfill my ambitions. I see a lot of others who haven't done as much as I have move upward rapidly and it bothers me a lot. I know this is affecting the quality of my work.

I have shown that I can grow in terms of responsibility and accountability. After a long stint at a company where I really believed that I would end my career, I was laid off and while I have landed on my feet, I am struggling to understand what it is that I actually can do! I have forgotten what drives me, what unique things I bring to the table. And since I am advancing into my late middle age, this is a scary prospect.

I am 50, and by all conventional measures, quite successful. I enjoy my co-workers, my teams respect me and I have achieved significant financial rewards. I guess I could accept this status quo and "coast" to retirement. Yet, I feel frightened at the prospect of not challenging myself and others, of not being passionate about my work as I once was, of suddenly being "mediocre."

I am an entrepreneur who has enjoyed good success in my first decade of business activity. Now things seem to be slumping, and I can't quite gather up the "mojo" I used to have. I constantly question my decisions now, and every setback is very hard to overcome mentally. Although my family is very loving, I suspect their patience is wearing thin toward me, as I stumble through my day.

These are serious, painful problems – they distract us from our path at work and can result in a largely unsatisfactory, unfulfilled work life.

A number of years ago, I was an internal consultant for the company I worked for. I enjoyed working with my co-workers and got along well with my boss. At that time, the company was in the midst of both business turmoil as well as disruptive technology. After the initial few months of enthusiasm and freshness, I felt myself slowly getting into a rut. I felt that I had a lot of new ideas to offer and that I could really initiate significant transformation. I wanted not only to showcase my ideas, but also to get my coworkers fired up and working toward the same objectives. I repeatedly met with my supervisor and kept pushing. She was very understanding and listened, but I felt that we never really got anywhere. My attitude at work began to worsen, and while I executed my tasks dutifully, I wasn't really focused on doing my best work. I longed to be visible, the "go-to" guy. I spent lots of time thinking about how to become that leader who could get these types of things done. I thought that maybe what I really needed to do was target being a supervisor myself. So, I focused my efforts on getting in front of my supervisor's manager and letting her know about my aspirations. I went nowhere.

It took me a few months of introspection and some long heart-to-heart discussions with a mentor to figure it out. What I realized was that I had become a follower of the "being" cult and not the "doing" movement. I became obsessed with the thoughts of becoming a "leader" and muddled along at an "acceptable" rate. I began to realize that to change the situation, I had to create action within myself. I realized that to thrive at my work, to move toward fulfillment, I had to "do" exceptional work and what I wanted to "be" would follow. I realized that leadership starts within, and is built on an ongoing set of relentless and focused *behaviors*. As I practiced them, my career vision changed; I had new goals that moved me toward fulfilling work and away from the minimum acceptable bar that I was trying to meet!

Today, I work with many individuals who are stuck in the cult of "being." My primary work with them involves, first and foremost, their acceptance to move toward the ethic of "doing."

Where does "leadership" fit into all of this? Isn't leadership something that is reserved for the lucky few who inhabit the rarefied air of the "C-suite"? We are used to the idea of the celebrity CEO as the charismatic leader – inspirational, and full of vision and directives that move us. Must we "limit" the promise of leadership to a chosen few, or is it available to the "rest" of us? How can companies and people adjust to the virulent nature of change that assaults us every day? How do we construct meaningful experiences at work so that we rise above mediocrity? And finally, how do we thrive and achieve fulfillment at work, and find relevance and contentment and a connection to a larger goal?

I firmly believe that leadership is available to all of us! As long as we view "it" as a set of daily sustainable and repeatable behaviors, we can all aspire to become leaders. I am not advocating that we will all become versions of Jack

Welch, Bill Gates or Steve Jobs. Far from it. Look, not all of us can become that "celebrity" CEO that everyone thinks is required to attain any real level of leadership. If you can, awesome job! But if you cannot, no one is stopping you from carving a daily leader's life. Ultimately, the goal is to thrive, perform at an exceptional level and find fulfillment.

Imagine, if you will:

As a new entrant to the workplace, you are fired up about going to work every day. You have made a smooth and successful transition from being a student to being a full-time worker in the economy. You are able to handle the tasks given to you with aplomb, and generally know where you are going. Your co-workers are beginning to look to you to help them through certain situations – not always, but it seems like these situations are increasing. You do have concerns about your pay, your boss and your team, but those never interfere with your daily behavior – you feel like you are performing at an exceptional level.

As a newly minted leader, you are supremely confident in your abilities and your recent accomplishments. You are not threatened by the superior workmanship of your team members. Your team members view you as a capable and strong frontline leader. They are comfortable discussing almost any situation with you, knowing that you will be firm but fair with them. You are generally comfortable in your relationship with your boss, and if you have concerns, know of discrete ways to air them out. Your boss views you as a star frontline leader and relies heavily on you, especially during crunch times.

As a mid-career, seasoned professional, you are very much

focused on enabling your teams to succeed. You have no problems receding into the background and letting your star team members take the credit. You strive to achieve personal and professional relationships with your team members, knowing that they spend more time at work during the day than at any other place. You are considered a key individual for succession planning, and major company initiatives find their way to you for implementation. You are cool and calm in most situations and have a team of strong frontline leaders. Your boss won't make any major moves without your consensus.

As an accomplished and successful professional or entrepreneur, you have suddenly regained the fire that used to burn within. You rediscover your passions, your inner drive that always fired you up. And you have shed all the people and behaviors that hold you back, as you engage in activities that you are completely committed to. You typically want to jump out of bed and go to work every day. You realize that time is your most valuable asset, and you prioritize your life accordingly.

As a senior leader, you are poised at or near the helm of your company. You are recognized within the company as a visionary with a strong people focus. Your customers are enthralled with you and your stakeholders support you consistently. Your organization looks to you for guidance and oversight, placing an implicit trust in you, which you faithfully uphold. You are proud of the organization you built and/or are stewarding. You work very closely with your future leaders and help them make necessary transformations. You encourage honest and open feedback, and have built a supportive culture throughout the hierarchy. You always show up.

These scenarios are examples of leaders who have "become" by "doing." They never focused on the "becoming" part, instead focusing on the "doing" part. They built upon a foundation of daily leadership behavior, which produced these outcomes. Based on my experience with individuals focused on exceptional outcomes and fulfillment at work, here is what they focused on:

- They got rid of the notion that "leadership is not for everyone" – they truly believe that leadership *is* for everyone.

- They also firmly believe that leadership has to start from inside – that is, from within ourselves. And the way we show it, use it, achieve benefits out of it – is through others. They understand that we can't serve others if we don't lead from within.

- They understand that leadership is best delivered as a set of daily behaviors – not just as something to **be**, but as something we **do**.

- They believe that a relentless and intense focus on exceptional performance is a pre-requisite for fulfilling work.

How do we then construct ourselves in this leadership mold? Is there a template for such a leader? Is it "all or nothing"? Or is there **a way**, **a process and a system** that we can follow? Why do some people at work seem fulfilled while others don't? You and I both know that fulfillment has nothing to do with the title they hold, or the money they earn. (In fact, it seems to be inversely proportional in a lot of cases!!!) Why do we follow some people even if they seemingly have no formal authority? Come to think of it, why do people follow you?

I want to share with you what has worked for my clients and for me. I believe that leadership can be distilled down into a set of behaviors. Most self-help and personal development is focused on getting us to change our "state" and put ourselves in a positive and affirmed mindset. I have no arguments with this – in fact, what you think, believe, and know will get you halfway there. But I know that there is always a gap between a general's tent and a soldier's trench. That gap can only be filled by action! Not just action – but systematic action. And systematic action can only be achieved by practicing a set of behaviors. Not affirmations or "positive" thinking, but daily behaviors. I am convinced that true fulfillment at work is a result of deep practice of behaviors.

So, it is quite simple. However, I am not going to make you think it is easy! Changing and practicing a set of behaviors that are new will be hard. But there are some secrets to it and I will share them with you in this book. This book is fashioned to be an active companion on your journey. I have designed it so that you can pick any behavior set you wish to work on and use that part of the book to practice. Each chapter, or "Leadership Secret" is designed to help you understand and focus on a specific leadership behavior. After reading a description of the leadership secret, you will use a worksheet to gauge and practice your own behaviors.

You can use the worksheets repeatedly, using your first attempt as a "baseline." I have referenced other tools and resources wherever applicable and relevant.

There is a logical flow to this book. You can pick and choose a certain section if that is the area you want to focus on. If you wish to follow the sequence that I have provided, that's great, too. This is a practical book that is firmly aimed at getting you to be exceptional and find fulfillment at work. Considering that we spend most of our waking hours at some type of "workplace" or other, and that most people still define themselves by what they do, I believe that we have a personal responsibility to find fulfillment at work. For most of us, workplace fulfillment bleeds into personal achievement and fulfillment as well. Let's get started on your path to exceptional work.

WHAT'S THE MAIN IDEA?

Peter Drucker defines mission as *"your statement of why you do what you do; your declared reason for being; your purpose."* Use the Personal Mission Statement Assessment to craft your own personal mission statement. This exercise will force you to rely on your "Why" as well as your core competencies to drive out your unique mission.

1

A PERSONAL MISSION STATEMENT

Do you have a personal mission statement? Peter Drucker defines mission as *"your statement of why you do what you do; your declared reason for being; your purpose."* For so many of us, the "why" is submerged under a deluge of practicality – both real and self-inflicted. We are where we are, we think, because of all the daily responsibilities we need to meet – of being a mother, a husband, a manager, a farmer, etc. It is easy to hide behind this veil of certainty. The challenge is to look inside first and be brave enough to understand your "why." An easy recipe for this is to articulate your personal mission statement. This can then drive your behaviors and shape your success and fulfillment at work.

Dan had spent 15+ years nurturing an information technology (IT) career. By most accounts he was successful – he provided for his family, he seemed competent and his team appreciated his work efforts. But something was missing. He wasn't charged up about getting to work every day. He also found that he could complete most of his work on auto-pilot

– without much engagement. He had this sneaky feeling that he was "meant for more." When his new manager came in, she understood that something was wrong right away. (Now, Dan got really lucky here, since this new manager was a true leader – exhibiting some of the leadership behaviors that we will address later in the book.) She made Dan introspect and used a profiling tool to push him to understand what his strengths were – what his "core" competencies were. He understood that his "why" was inexplicably linked to what he thought his "core" was. He then evaluated how he could achieve his desired target "state" using his core competencies. He figured out an action statement, which encapsulated his reason for work. He found out that he still loved IT work. He just didn't wish to lead teams anymore (which is what he was doing at his current job). He had moved away from what he felt really fired him up (his "why" for working) – designing and building software that helped physically challenged people. His manager counseled him that while their company wasn't going after the physically challenged market, they could certainly help Dan with the "designing and building" part. She told Dan that if he was willing, she could move him to a role where he focused on design. The only caveat, she said, was that if Dan took this role, he would no longer be a team leader, but would have to work as an individual contributor. Dan decided to risk it. He jumped into the new role with gusto and excelled at it. Eventually, he found himself at an organization that indeed built software for the target market he wanted to serve. All of this happened because he started with an understanding of the "why" and a personal mission statement.

A personal mission statement stops you from meandering

along in your career. It takes the focus away from titles, corporate ladder climbing and petty politics. Instead, it focuses you sharply on achievement, empowerment and fulfillment. Without a definition of why you want to strive, and what the outcome of your striving is – it is pointless to string together a long career, entirely focused on the next promotion.

Use the Personal Mission Statement Assessment to craft your own personal mission statement. Remember, your mission statement is your own. It doesn't have to impress anyone else – it just has to be yours! You can share it with others or keep it private. However, this is the time to unveil your inner drive – so if you fudge here, you are only misleading yourself. Leaders on their way to fulfillment are true to themselves first.

This exercise will force you to rely on your "why" as well as your core competencies to drive out your unique mission.

Exercise # 1

A PERSONAL MISSION STATEMENT

1. Figure out your Core, first. What is the set of Core Competencies that you excel in? Have you visualized and articulated it for yourself?

Identify at least 5 Core Competencies that you either excel in or wish to:

Core Competency # 1: _____

Core Competency # 2: _____

Core Competency # 3: _____

Core Competency # 4: _____

Core Competency # 5: _____

2. Figure out the Outcome, next. Leveraging your Core, what do you wish to achieve? What is your "target state"?

Identify (write it in a narrative or a bulleted list) what you wish your Outcome to be:

_____

_____

_____

_____

_____

_____

3. Craft your personal mission. With Core as the starting point and the Outcome as the desired state, develop your "how-to" – your personal mission statement. It should (a) tell you and others what you wish to do, (b) identify how you will do it, and (c) give you a clear picture of how it will help you find fulfillment.

In this section, write about (a) what you wish to achieve, (b) how you will achieve it, and (c) why this end goal or target is important to your fulfillment:

_____

_____

_____

_____

_____

_____

In this section, pull it all together and write your personal mission statement:

_____

_____

_____

_____

_____

_____

WHAT'S THE MAIN IDEA?

THE LEADERSHIP ASCENT CURVE illustrates the ascent of a leader through the various levels of leadership. It is based on a foundation I call the Leadership Launch Platform. There are four levels in the Leadership Ascent Curve: The Seeker, The Expert, The Enabler and The Transformer. Moving up this ascent curve requires you to focus on the four building blocks of your Leadership Launch Platform:

1. Acquire – Core Skills

2. Accomplish – Initiatives

3. Achieve – Credibility

4. Nurture & Leverage – Relationships

2

Leadership Secret # 2

BUILD YOUR LEADERSHIP LAUNCH PLATFORM

In today's world of the goal to "become someone" rather than to "do something," leadership becomes a façade rather than a behavior. A much better way is to stand on what I call your own "Leadership Launch Platform." Why not stand on a sustainable model of leadership behavior within ourselves so that we can, in fact, lead others? Why not be more substance than form? It is straightforward, not easy – just simple! The Leadership Ascent Curve provides you with that framework, the roadmap for your journey toward exceptional outcomes and fulfillment.

What is the Leadership Ascent Curve? It is a model and a system toward sustainable leadership behaviors. The Leadership Ascent Curve illustrates the ascent of a leader through the various levels of leadership. It is based on a foundation called the Leadership Launch Platform. As you can see, there are four levels: The Seeker, The Expert, The Enabler and The Transformer. Moving up this ascent curve requires you to focus on the building blocks of your Leadership Launch Platform.

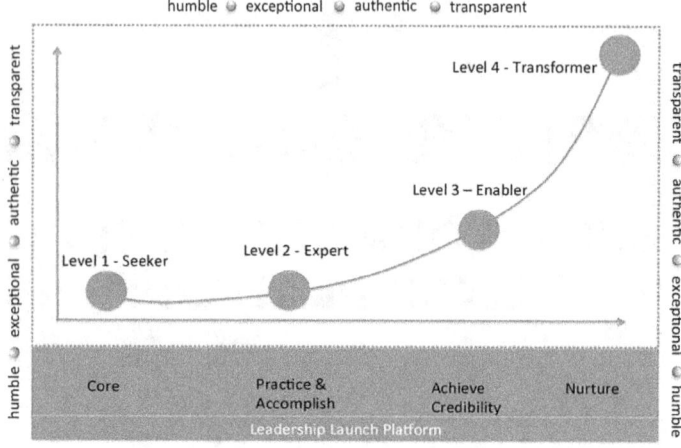

You may already be on your way, or you may be constructing your platform. The reality is that these four building blocks require constant feeding and care – you are never "done." It is an ongoing commitment to yourself. Commit to these four building blocks and embrace leadership as a daily behavior, and you are sure to do exceptional work and thrive in today's workplace:

1. Acquire – Core Skills

The basic and essential core of any leader is, first and foremost, competence. Whatever your chosen field is, commit to a relentless pursuit and mastery of those core skills. An incompetent leader is a pretender, at best. Leaders who are at this stage of the ascent are typically Level 1 leaders – "Seekers." They have a fully developed personal mission statement. They know what their core should be made up of and they tirelessly build it up by acquiring skills and knowledge.

2. Accomplish – Initiatives

Your competence and core skills need to drive you to *finish* projects. This is key – the starting and finishing of purposeful work, where you are able to use and polish your core skills. Whether you are starting off, changing careers, adding skills, or taking on more responsibility, this is a key building block to the foundation of your platform. Leaders who are at this stage of the ascent are typically Level 2 leaders – "Experts." In addition to being Seekers, Experts have begun to finish initiatives and are sought-after, "go-to" resources in their communities. They lead and are put in leadership roles due to complete mastery in their specific areas.

3. Achieve – Credibility

You are credible based on what you accomplish – whether it is a set of outcomes you generate or a set of outcomes you enable in others. Credibility is a result, not an action. It appears, as if by magic, once you actively pursue the first two building blocks. Leaders who are at this stage of the ascent are typically Level 3 leaders – "Enablers." At this level, leaders are no longer looking to solve problems based solely on their functional expertise. They are now leveraging the strengths of others to solve organizational issues. They understand that to empower others, they no longer need to be the "smartest person in the room." While lesser leaders shrink from giving others visibility and power, Level 3 leaders are always focused on ensuring the success of those around them.

4. Nurture & Leverage – Relationships

You now collaborate, connect, and engage yourself and others toward a higher level of performance. This is the zone where you can launch not only yourself, but others as well. You begin to see and understand that the leadership **behavior within yourself** now actually results in **outcomes for others** – the others whom you lead and who have chosen to follow you. Leaders who are at this stage of the ascent are typically Level 4 leaders – "Transformers." At this level, the entire value that these leaders bring is to focus on totally transforming the people they lead. They are completely focused on getting their people to their highest possible level of performance. Level 4 leaders do not shirk the attributes of the Seeker, the Expert or the Enabler – in fact, they will use those attributes within themselves whenever necessary, but always in the service of transforming someone else to a peak performance state, so that ultimately the entire whole achieves fulfillment.

Exercise # 2

BUILD YOUR LEADERSHIP
LAUNCH PLATFORM

So, here are four simple rituals to infuse into your weekly calendar. Schedule them in as though they were specific activities. Look at them every morning and discipline yourself to practice them. Look at them again at the end of the week and check them off if you have completed them. The idea here is to bake these rituals into your routine so that they become a pattern of behavior. These behaviors will lead you to exceptional performance and fulfillment. This system is based on my work with superb leaders for the past 20+ years. It works for them. It definitely works for me and I fervently hope it provides you with a guiding path as well. Here they are:

1. Design Your Core:
In an environment where the packaging sometimes seems to overshadow the content, it is even more important to focus on identifying and focusing on your Core Competencies. What is it that you bring to the table? Do you keep it fresh? How do you use it daily? Are you recognized because of it? If not, what are you doing about it???? As a Level 1 leader, The Seeker should be intent on designing his or her Core.

- Have you crafted your personal mission statement?

- If you have, review it and make sure you know what your Core is.

- If you know what your Core is, make sure you nurture it and transfer that potential into your work.

- **Key Question for the week:** By following this ritual, you should be able to answer: "What will you bring to the table this week that will leverage your unique value?"

_____

_____

_____

_____

_____

2. Fire it Up:

I love this quote from Phil Jackson — .... "After coaching him for eight seasons, I still marvel at how much Michael's enthusiasm energizes us, even at practice. I mean he never takes a day off..."

The point is to keep your Core fresh and relevant; you not only have to constantly learn, you also have to practice your craft; and, you have to find ways to do that with intensity and with regularity. Are you? As a Level 2 leader, The Expert is intent on firing up his Core.

- Based on your Core, if you haven't already identified key activities that showcase it – then please do so.

- Have you aligned your goals and patterns to fit your core? If so, what activities will serve to enable these patterns?

- **Key Question for the week:** By following this ritual you should be able to answer: "How will you practice the activity you identified above?"

_____

_____

_____

_____

_____

3. Achieve Credibility:

If you are leading with H.E.A.T. – by being humble, exceptional, authentic and transparent, and you are focused on accomplishing outcomes, credibility will chase you! As a Level 3 leader, The Enabler is using credibility to drive further up the Leadership Ascent Curve.

- By crafting your goals and activities to align with your Core and personal mission statement, you have set yourself up for a system and process to succeed. Now, you have to ensure that you can accomplish initiatives that bring value to your team, your department, and your organization. To do this, you have to sell your unique value to your environment.

- **Key Question for the week:** By following this ritual, you should be able to answer: "What will you accomplish (finish) this week that will utilize your unique competencies?"

_____

_____

_____

_____

_____

4. Nurture & Transform:

You are in the "zone" – you have the tools and credibility built on the inside, to really serve others on the outside. You are completely focused on the impact you can create by helping others achieve and accomplish; you are truly at the pinnacle of leadership. As a Level 4 leader, The Transformer is intent on serving others and multiplying the benefits of his or her own leadership.

- The platinum standard of leadership is, of course, to selflessly enable others to excel. By focusing on your personal leadership that comes from within, you can help others to propel themselves to perform at an exceptional level.

- **Key Question for the week:** By following this ritual, you should be able to answer: "How will you ensure that someone else on your team will benefit in a tangible way because of your behavior?"

_____

_____

_____

_____

WHAT'S THE MAIN IDEA?

While climbing the Leadership Ascent Curve takes you ever higher into the realms of effective leadership, you have to do it in the right way. A great and effective leader always leads with H.E.A.T. – by being humble, exceptional, authentic and transparent.

3

LEAD WITH H.E.A.T. – BY BEING HUMBLE, EXCEPTIONAL, AUTHENTIC AND TRANSPARENT

To climb the Leadership Ascent Curve (Leadership Secret # 2) – and to do it the right way – you have to lead by being Humble, Exceptional, Authentic and Transparent. This is the overall umbrella that you have to model your leadership behaviors on. I remember a past client who said that on his way up his own ascent curve, he had made so many enemies, he had destroyed so many relationships that he wondered if there was a better way. I believe that behaving with H.E.A.T. – that is, by being humble, exceptional, authentic and transparent – is a better way.

HUMBLE

"The fullest and best ears of corn hang lowest toward the ground." - BISHOP REYNOLDS

Today, the workplace puts immense pressure on us to perform, to deliver value. We are (and should be) measured by the results we achieve. There is a premium placed on initiative and the ability to lead oneself and others. None of this translates to the need to be arrogant – to display a total disregard to the people around you and the way they work – to hide certain innate weaknesses under the guise of hard-charging "single mindedness." And yet, the landscape is littered with the excesses of arrogant leaders – leading teams, companies, even countries into situations where alienation of the people around them is commonplace. The evidence is damning, too – these same leaders are falling, often bringing down the very organizations they were appointed to lead.

Humility as a daily leadership behavior may be rare, but ought to be even more significant in today's workplace. If we accept that leadership is about enabling positive outcomes for others around us, then a daily leadership behavior we can all exhibit is to serve with humility. To me, humility as a daily leadership behavior means:

- Remember that those around you (whether peers, subordinates, or bosses) are people with their own egos, aspirations, desires, families, strengths, weaknesses and maybe a secret predilection for eating vanilla ice cream at midnight (no...that's not mine!!). When you have this "empathy light" switched on, it is difficult to use arrogance as a leadership style – you realize that you are dealing with living, breathing people, with all that comes with it.

- Show your team/peers/etc. that you are not *above* a task or activity. I had the pleasure of working with a senior leader in a large corporation who wouldn't balk at jumping in and helping to complete last-minute meeting logistics and preparation. He would then assume the role of primary presenter, and the impact he had on his team was priceless. No one ever shirked any task, as long as they were all convinced that it led them to the outcome that was being expected.

- A number of my clients are ultra-high achievers with high IQs. Most of them buy and sell ideas, so the person with the right idea is always the king of the jungle. This is what brought them initial success; however, most of them find that it doesn't seem to get them to the next level. Even armed with this knowledge, they find it difficult to change their behavior with their teams. It is not sufficient to open a meeting, dictate that each member present their viewpoint, and then proceed to tell them that your own idea was the best idea anyway. If you do this, then why bother considering anything else? A true characteristic of humility is to be able to let people air out their viewpoints and be able to include those ideas in any type of resultant action. An idea so built on multiple pillars will be more successfully executed than an arrogant leader's unilateral mandates.

I know it is in every one of us to show humility, because as human beings we are constantly striving to connect with others and reach for something larger, something that provides us relevance. You have to be humble and add it to your portfolio of leadership behaviors.

EXCEPTIONAL

A long time ago, I was an undergraduate student studying mechanical engineering in a college and university known for academic rigor and excellence. When we entered school, all of us, regardless of our majors, had to go through a semester of "woodworking" and a semester of what was termed "fitting" (also known amongst the incoming group of students as "torture"!). Fitting was about becoming familiar with metalworking and the tolerances between moving parts.

Well, this workshop class was usually the last one in my daily schedule and after

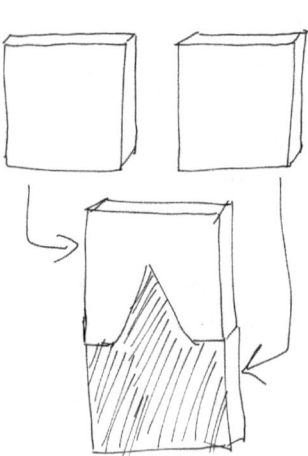

being beat up mentally for four to five hours prior, I thought this ought to be a breeze. The very first session went something like this: All of us were handed two square metal pieces, about 2 inches by 2 inches, and about a quarter-inch thick. We were told to cut out a pattern and make these two pieces "fit."

We proceeded to hacksaw the metal pieces (after measuring the pattern) and got to the general shapes fairly quickly. "Well," we thought, "this engineering stuff isn't too bad." So, one by one we walked over to the workshop foreman (who was the rough equivalent of a Gunnery Sergeant Major in any army, as we later found out) who asked us to "fit" the two pieces together and hold it up to the window through which the late winter sun was filtering through. He said, "Look, you can still see sunlight coming through the crack, so here, take this file and get the edges down so they fit right." "How hard could this be," we thought, "just smooth out the edges and we are home free!"

Well, even after hours of filing, sunlight always seemed to find a way out. (Later we were to learn that a first-time workshop student had zero chance of achieving the machine-like "tolerance" he was looking for.) We filed away for two hours (anyone who's filed metal to achieve tolerances can bear me out on this; it is not the most pleasant of tasks – most definitely not for college freshmen) and the class ended. He smiled and said, "Oh, you can always do it next session, as we are not moving beyond this until I sign off." Two weeks later, he eased up and said that we'd never build/make/design anything worthwhile if we didn't understand the need to be fine-tuned and micro-intense in our work.

He taught me a valuable lesson that day: to achieve exceptional work, there is no letup. That regardless of the role we play, the title we hold, the position we aspire to – we'd better keep our eye on the small things, and the big things will follow suit.

Footnote – every single one of my classmates from that

day 30 years ago is super successful by any yardstick in today's world. We had many bricklayers lay our foundation those four years, and I think this was one of the very first.

AUTHENTIC

Not long ago, I worked with a client (I don't advise him anymore, and you'll see why!) who had bought into the leadership mantra of "telling stories" to deliver his message. Not a bad idea at all. Except that, in addition to being an abusive leader given to frequent, entirely unprofessional outbursts at his staff, this guy told stories and used metaphors that were not authentic at all.

Case in point, he used a story about a ship being fired upon in war as a metaphor to illustrate multiple challenges that faced his business unit. And, he related how a battleship responds to the furious pace of war. And of course – he fashioned himself the Admiral, and his staff as the gunners....

A great inspirational tool, you say? The problem was, he had never served, and most of his staff knew about this! The message came across as so incredibly hollow, it fell on deaf ears – and his team did not respond as expected.

I think storytelling is a great tool in getting a point across and moving the dial. However, to be effective, you have to be authentic. It is incredibly arrogant to assume that using "packaged," "off-the-shelf" stories can influence your teams. That is putting a very low expectation on your team, and that is definitely not a daily leadership behavior. I have worked with authentic leaders who used anecdotes, experiences and real-life stories that they personally lived through, and I have seen them rouse their teams to become energized and focused on the outcomes at hand. Here is a technique that is fast, fun and, I hope, educational to help you along this path:

Own the message, not the delivery. Try this: Compose emails as usual in your regular workday. But, before sending them off to your colleagues, send them to yourself. Not a blind copy – put yourself in the "To" field. Do the same with the voice mails you want to send to your team. So, in essence, you are changing the "From" to the "To." Read/listen to your voice. Measure it along these lines: Is it authentic? Are you standing on a firm platform of your own achievements/accomplishments/credibility? Would this help the recipient move the dial and own the outcome? Be honest about your appraisal and you will begin practicing this daily leadership behavior of being authentic.

TRANSPARENT

A few years ago, I worked for a firm with a global footprint at a reasonably (or so I thought) high organizational level. All that meant was that a number of people looked to me to communicate to them about the goings on at Corporate. Well, this firm had reached a point where the senior officers were seriously considering being acquired. However, there was no real communication about this consideration – which I guess is understandable – since there was nothing concrete on the table. At a certain point that year a news agency in one of the countries we operated in broke the news about an impending merger with the name of a mega corporation as the acquirer. Suddenly, there was a rush of activity and a circling of wagons at our firm. Since the news item was already out there, our executives were forced to communicate...and they did. They denied all rumors and stated that we were financially very healthy (we were), and that we had a long-term organic growth strategy (which we didn't) and that there were no immediate plans for a merger. Less than three months later we were acquired. A number of senior folks like me left with a bad taste. Maybe we would have left anyway, even if the plans had been more transparent, but we wouldn't have felt that we were lied to. My level of respect for some of the individuals involved took a deep dive. While this anecdote may be a macro-level incident, issues of transparency arise every day at each level of an organization. I remember when my supervisors and managers (drowning in the business vernacular of the day) would talk about "need to know" and "information gate-keeping." If protecting and obfuscating information was the source of power in those days, the same is not true today! If you exhibit this behavior as a leader today, you will lose the power and influence you need over your tribe and community (read: your teams!). You can build a platform of power and influence through your competencies, achievements, expertise and relationships. You cannot grow or serve if you hide and protect. So, be transparent – even if it is painful in the short term, you will gain in the long run.

Use the H.E.A.T. Self-Assessment to find out how "hot" your leadership is. Remember – the more honest you are, the easier it will be to fill the gap between where you are and where you want to be. And this exercise is not a one-time activity. Use it constantly to check and align your leadership behaviors.

Exercise # 3

LEAD WITH H.E.A.T.

H.E.A.T. SELF-ASSESSMENT

Think about your behavior at work and select the most relevant statement.

HUMBLE

1. I make sure that I listen to everyone's opinion in my team.

Strongly Disagree   **Strongly Agree**
   ◯   ◯   ◯   ◯   ◯
   1   2   3   4   5

2. I am able to accept other people's ideas without rancor.

Strongly Disagree   **Strongly Agree**
   ◯   ◯   ◯   ◯   ◯
   1   2   3   4   5

3. I recognize that each team member is unique and brings different strengths.

Strongly Disagree   **Strongly Agree**
   ◯   ◯   ◯   ◯   ◯
   1   2   3   4   5

4. I am flexible in performing whatever task is required for ultimate team success.

Strongly Disagree   **Strongly Agree**
   ◯   ◯   ◯   ◯   ◯
   1   2   3   4   5

5. I use title and authority only as a last resort.

Strongly Disagree   Strongly Agree

◯   ◯   ◯   ◯   ◯
1   2   3   4   5

EXCEPTIONAL

1. I strive to raise the bar constantly – both for myself as well as for my team.

Strongly Disagree   Strongly Agree

◯   ◯   ◯   ◯   ◯
1   2   3   4   5

2. I strive to understand the details of my work and excel in as many of them as possible.

Strongly Disagree   Strongly Agree

◯   ◯   ◯   ◯   ◯
1   2   3   4   5

3. I cultivate, nurture and intensely focus on collaborative relationships.

Strongly Disagree   Strongly Agree

◯   ◯   ◯   ◯   ◯
1   2   3   4   5

4. I focus on outstanding outcomes, without regard to status or hierarchy.

Strongly Disagree   Strongly Agree

◯   ◯   ◯   ◯   ◯
1   2   3   4   5

5. I am ready to do "whatever it takes" when my team needs me to.

Strongly Disagree   Strongly Agree

◯   ◯   ◯   ◯   ◯
1   2   3   4   5

AUTHENTIC

1. I use true personal experiences and anecdotes to motivate and illustrate, and avoid clichés.

2. I am openly passionate about the specific topics that I care most about.

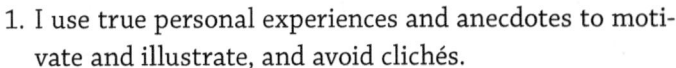

3. I am consistent in participation – in both good and bad situations.

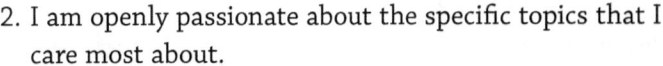

4. I am frank about my weaknesses.

Strongly Disagree   Strongly Agree

○   ○   ○   ○   ○

1   2   3   4   5

5. My words and actions are aligned.

Strongly Disagree   Strongly Agree

○   ○   ○   ○   ○

1   2   3   4   5

TRANSPARENT

1. I am open and straightforward about information that can help my team.

Strongly Disagree   Strongly Agree

○   ○   ○   ○   ○

1   2   3   4   5

2. I make sure that implicit and explicit agendas are properly communicated and understood.

Strongly Disagree   Strongly Agree
  ◯   ◯   ◯   ◯   ◯
  1   2   3   4   5

3. I make sure that my team is aware of my personal goals.

Strongly Disagree   Strongly Agree
  ◯   ◯   ◯   ◯   ◯
  1   2   3   4   5

4. I share my excitement as well as my disappointments.

Strongly Disagree   Strongly Agree
  ◯   ◯   ◯   ◯   ◯
  1   2   3   4   5

5. I handle conflicts directly and respectfully.

Strongly Disagree   Strongly Agree
  ◯   ◯   ◯   ◯   ◯
  1   2   3   4   5

Scoring: This is a count of your 4s and 5s. Not the sum of the individual scores.

17 OR MORE (number of 4 and 5s)
RED HOT – Congratulations. You are running hot! Don't be complacent. Leadership is a daily behavior and you need to H.E.A.T. it up every day.

15 – 16 (number of 4 and 5s)
HOT – You are on the way to achieving peak leadership behavior. Focus on your strengths, nurture your relationships and spend more time enabling others.

10 – 14 (number of 4 and 5s)
WARM – You are beginning to realize that leadership is a behavior that you need to practice every day. Continue what you have begun and increase your focus on serving others.

9 OR FEWER (number of 4 and 5s)
LUKE WARM – Be honest with yourself. Solicit team member opinions about what you can do to help them and then act on 2-3 things daily. You will be heating up in no time!

WHAT'S THE MAIN IDEA?

"Get action, do things; be sane; don't fritter away your time; create, act, take a place wherever you are and be somebody: get action." (In Richard Hofstadter, *The American Political Tradition: And the Men Who Made it, 1948)*

It is imperative to focus on forward progress in your projects and activities.

4

THE FLYING RUBBER BAND

Stretch a rubber band and it has *potential* – let it go and it can *fly*! The value you want to create for yourself, your team or the world at large is kinetic. The potential that you and your ideas have does not translate into value until you take action. Action is aptly described here by Theodore Roosevelt:

"Get action, do things; be sane; don't fritter away your time; create, act, take a place wherever you are and be somebody: get action." (In Richard Hofstadter, The American Political Tradition: And the Men Who Made it, 1948)

It is imperative to focus on forward progress in your projects and activities.

I work with managers and individual contributors who have the right intent to move forward, the right attitude to collaborate – but never close the deal. The right intent does not translate into positive results. To achieve value, you have to force yourself into action – however far that takes you out of your comfort zone.

One of the most common excuses preventing people from something that they "ought" to do is "I don't have enough time." Every other excuse revolves around this one ("If only I had the money to do it…", "I have a full family schedule – no time do that," "I wish I had the talent to do that," "Well….she was born into that anyway," etc., etc.). What is fascinating indeed is that there is the same finite time available to everyone – those who succeed as well as those who choose not to. Successful people just seem to find that time to go after what they want.

The best real-life "ordinary people" example is this – talk to anyone who has lost a lot of weight and started living a healthy lifestyle. Living a healthy lifestyle requires a time commitment – the time to exercise, the time to focus on the right foods and the time to focus away from the wrong foods! So, how do they achieve it? How do they find this time that was essentially missing before? I was talking to someone very close to me recently about this topic. She had struggled with weight and illness after childbirth, but managed to change her direction after almost 10 years by finding that extra time to live a healthy lifestyle. I asked her how she made this shift. She told me that her mental model was always that you had to "exercise for one continuous hour each day" to achieve any real benefit. Since she never could find that one contiguous hour, she never exercised. "So, what changed?" I asked. She replied that she met her physical trainer (by chance!) who asked her, "Why do you need sixty minutes all at one time? Why not three minutes at a time?" Well, that was a revelation! The final boundary that this woman crossed was when she told me, "I permitted myself to abandon the arbitrary sixty-minute barrier and found multiple short periods of time that I was able to use." Today she is fitter than she ever was and is even helping others with wellness advice. The lesson for me here is that transformation and change are big ideas that require little steps. They happen in small seismic events that then trigger that massive leap you are looking for. If you want to turbo charge your career – find those three minutes! Work on what you really want to do in smaller "timelets" throughout the day or week or month. Permit yourself to abandon needless and arbitrary constraints. You have just increased your chance at success.

Action requires preparation and thought. What it does *not* require is talk! So, without further ado, complete the exercise for this chapter – and you will soon launch into action!

Exercise # 4

THE FLYING RUBBER BAND

List the Top 5 things you have been worrying about or wishing you wanted to do and for which you never "found time," or have been waiting for some other event to happen before you would attempt these, or have been scared of doing because of what others may feel/think/say:

A.

1. _____

2. _____

3. _____

4. _____

5. _____

B.

Strike out 3 of these Top 5. Not that they are unimportant – but force yourself to pick what is absolutely essential. These are things that will push you toward your desired target and fulfill your personal mission statement. Be ruthless.

C.

For each of the Top 2 items remaining, list 5 Action Items you will perform this week. (Do this exercise on a Sunday – so you will have a complete week.)

1. _____

a. _____

b. _____

c. _____

d. _____

e. _____

2 _____

   a. _____

   b. _____

   c. _____

   d. _____

   e. _____

D.

Schedule 1a through 1e and 2a through 2e into your time management device of choice (paper, electronic, whatever). And then, just complete these activities as they show up on your schedule. No extra talk, no additional thought. Do this for 21 days. Research has shown that to acquire a new habit, it takes 21 days of practice. In the grand scheme of things, what's 21 days? You will be amazed to realize that as you perform the activities that really matter to you, your outlook, demeanor, and – most excitingly – your results begin to match your idea of who you are and where you wish to be.

WHAT'S THE MAIN IDEA?

A fulfilled leader "leans into" the issue at hand and pushes it/tackles it/pays the tax now, instead of waiting for a future disaster. It's all in the now – for you to own the outcome of your endeavor, you have to practice the daily leadership behavior of "leaning into it and pushing," rather than the oh-so-much-easier shoulder shrug.

When you get embroiled in a negative conversation, you have to take responsibility to get it around to a positive path as soon as possible. You will see that the other person(s) will react by getting drawn/pulled out of the negative, as if drawn by a magnet. The secret is to seek a ray of potential positive outcome in the situation and pull the group along.

We are all shaped by our pasts, one way or the other – however, there is a tremendous price we pay when we are bound by our pasts… Use your platform of past successes to fly free, not be tethered.

5

MAKE INERTIA YOUR ENEMY – OR HOW TO BE A CATALYST FOR FORWARD MOVEMENT

Nancy was frustrated. She felt she was in meetings all day that never "went anywhere." Most of the discussions, or chatter, really focused on the unreasonable demands being made by senior management. When she started meetings with agendas for upcoming work, attendees frequently got lost in how the existing politics were just not going to enable them to execute, of how things were just not going to work. She was unable to direct the participants to any kind of productive discussions.

While her company was doing quite well, a lot of her team interactions seemed to be stuck. Her group was viewed as steady, if a bit dull and risk averse. With a change in the senior leadership at her internal client, there were a lot of aggressive demands for more service from her group. She found herself frequently protecting the existing or old ways of doing things, protecting the old systems that ran the business processes, to a point where her new customers were getting frustrated. She sensed this and wanted to figure out how to solve this problem. I worked with Nancy over a year to help her find the right solutions for her situation. We were able to formulate some key strategies that moved her past these obstacles. Nancy went from strength to strength and today is a valued member of senior management at her company. Here, then, are the strategies that proved successful:

Strategy # 1 – Don't shrug it off . . . .Lean into it! Move that dial now . . . . .or pay the tax later

"That's the way it is…"; "She's just that way – that is a given…"; "You know it's not going to work, but what can we do?" You know it: the classic shoulder shrug, the feeling of a massive uphill climb, and our default reaction of *inertia*.

The problem with the shrug is this: you know that it's going to come back to bite you! It's always a case of paying your tax up front, or, paying a huge penalty later – especially in today's climate, where there is such a fear of job longevity and the huge pressure to just go along and stay safe – it is all the more natural for us to stay in our zones of inertia.

Why don't you "lean into" the issue at hand and push it/ tackle it/pay the tax now, instead of waiting for a future disaster? It's all in the now – for you to own the outcome of your endeavor, you have to practice the daily leadership behavior of "leaning into it and pushing," rather than the oh-so-much-easier shoulder shrug.

Strategy # 2 – Be a magnet, pull the negative OUT: The magic of the positive pull

I'm sure we have all been culprits of this – the soothing blanket of whining and moaning, what my Aussie cricket friends call whinging. You know what I'm talking about, right? And it gets even better if you are able to harmonize it with a couple of other team members adding their chorus! Here's the thing – you can do that to blow off some steam (good), or continue to depress yourself and your team (bad)! Definitely not a daily leadership behavior – not going to get you into that "exceptional" zone we want you to be in.

Here's what I have found – when you get embroiled in a negative conversation you have to take responsibility to get it around to a positive path as soon as possible. You will see that the other person(s) will react by getting drawn/pulled out of the negative, as if drawn by a magnet. The secret is to seek a ray of potential positive outcome in the situation and pull the group along. This is not even a choice for those of us who wish to practice daily leadership behavior – it is simply the way we have to lead and move ourselves to exceptional performance.

Strategy # 3 – Checking stuff at the door & other voluntary actions – Volunteer to free your mind...

We have beefs about our work/our team/our bosses/our pay. Okay, I get it. And I am sure that most of us are taking some active steps to address one or more of these issues. But here's the thing – how many of us are able to check this stuff at the door when we focus on the outcomes that are expected of us? "Above my pay grade" or "We need more leadership around here" could be statements that maybe ought to be reflected back to us. How do we balance these emotional responses with our resolve to practice leadership behavior daily?

Here's the daily leadership behavior action plan for one day. Check this stuff at the door when you enter your workplace – just put it in coat check, get a ticket – so you can claim it back on the way out. And think about your favorite volunteer organization that you are fired up about. Go through your meetings/interactions/tasks with the same passion. I assure you – you will have an exceptional day. And, you will forget to claim that stuff you checked in... Will this behavior address your underlying issues with your workplace? My answer is that combating them with exceptional performance is, by far, the best option available to you – either to surmount them or to launch into your next phase.

P.S. – look, if you believe that you are in the wrong place/ wrong time/wrong set of people – are you taking steps to untether yourself? If not, then the next strategy addresses that – but if you believe that you are in the right place, but still get bogged down from being an exceptional performer – then, there is no excuse but to follow this daily leadership behavior.

Strategy # 4 – Of Safety Blankets and Tethers – Get stuck OR Jump off that platform of yours ...

It is very reasonable to expect that one stands on one's accomplishments. To feel credible and respected because of your existing work portfolio is indeed something we all aspire to. But today's business landscape demands quickness and flexibility. When our bosses/stakeholders/ customers entrust us with that "next" big responsibility, they are looking at the outcome you achieved and how you achieved it – not necessarily the system or the process or the transaction you now own.

My work with leaders and superstar employees sometimes finds me with people who just won't let go – of the system they built/of the process they designed/etc. – even if that next responsibility/goal dictates a change in direction/strategy. It is that safety blanket that tethers us to the past, when what we really need is to launch into the future.

So, a key action that we need to take as daily leaders is to leverage the results and the "hows" of past successes, not to circle the wagons and hang on to that safety blanket.

We are all shaped by our pasts, one way or the other – however, there is a tremendous price we pay when we are bound by our pasts… Use your platform of past successes to fly free, not be tethered.

Exercise # 5

MAKE INERTIA YOUR ENEMY – OR HOW TO BE A CATALYST FOR FORWARD MOVEMENT.

1. List one "insurmountable" obstacle at work. It could be a company policy, a peer, an employee direct report, a boss, a project situation, etc.

2. List 5 small activities you will do *this* week to address the obstacle you identified. Don't be over-awed by the magnitude of the problem; just turn the focus inward and affirm what you can do:

   a. _____

   b. _____

   c. _____

   d. _____

   e. _____

3. Identify 5 potential negative / discouraging situations you may encounter at work this week, and develop a positive response to each:

Potential Situation	Your Planned Response

4. Moving forward, and getting unstuck:

Reflect on your biggest past success in your job:_____

_____

_____

_____

List (and be honest now!) what you really think that success means today – visualize that success in a simple statement.: _____

_____

_____

_____

List your current behavior with your peers/cross-functional teams/bosses:

_____

_____

_____

_____

And finally, take an honest inventory – how many of these behaviors are about protecting your safety blanket? How many aren't? Those numbers ought to tell you what you should be doing... or not doing!

WHAT'S THE MAIN IDEA?

How about if we all tried to simply "break our own records" for the day? Faced with seemingly insurmountable challenges, what if we simply looked inward first, stretched ourselves just a bit more than usual, focused just that much more today, compared to yesterday, on leading ourselves and others without regard to position or status?

6

BREAK YOUR OWN RECORD.

At one of my son's band concerts, his band teacher asked the audience to acknowledge several of his students who had auditioned for an all-region band. When the applause died down, he said, "Auditioning for the all-region band is not necessarily about getting selected; it is more about breaking your own record." What he was alluding to, of course, was the fact that the students had to stretch up, choose two pieces that were quite challenging to them, and try to accomplish playing the pieces. He was trying to get them to "break their own record" of ability, accomplishment and comfort zones. What a fascinating idea – and, I think, just perfect as a daily leadership behavior.

At work, as we are faced with daunting challenges/tasks/ people, the end point or the *outcome point*, as I prefer to call it, can look insurmountable. Project deadlines can look unreasonable, breaking through people barriers can seem impossible and that feeling of helplessness can quickly become overwhelming.

How about if we all tried to simply "break our own records" for the day? Faced with seemingly insurmountable challenges, what if we simply looked inward first, stretched ourselves just a bit more than usual, focused just that much more today, compared to yesterday, on leading ourselves and others without regard to position or status? And to keep it simple – just identify three to five actions that you will break your own record on for today, and I guarantee this – you will come out with a sense of accomplishment that will make that insurmountable challenge that much less daunting. Build a "portfolio" of record-breaking days like this and you are well on your way to becoming exceptional!

Exercise # 6

BREAK YOUR OWN RECORD.

1. Identify 3 to 5 actions that you will "break your own record" on for this week.

   a. _____

   b. _____

   c. _____

   d. _____

   e. _____

2. At the end of the week, take a few minutes to evaluate your "portfolio." How did you do? Did you stretch and excel? Were you able to break out of a limit that you had set previously? Did you break your own record?

WHAT'S THE MAIN IDEA?

The next time you move into "design" from "idea," check your *structure* and *content*. Be unflagging in the former and flexible in the latter.

7

COLLABORATING FOR EXECUTION - WHEN TO HOLD & WHEN TO FOLD

Ideas can come from anywhere. The premium is really during the execution phase of any initiative you are involved in. And a core leadership behavior during execution is collaborative progress – the art and science of leveraging the strengths of many to achieve the promises of an idea or vision.

Frequently, I see a significant roadblock early in the transition from idea/vision to repeatable and sustainable execution. Let's call it the "design" phase – when key teams get involved in translating ideas into a tangible product or service that leads to the ultimate outcomes that everyone desires. A lot of us make up our minds on how this translation should happen, fill in the details in our minds (and maybe even on paper), and then won't budge from that stance when we encounter (predictably) the push and pull of creative cross purposes of others in the team. I firmly believe that the cracks in any project begin to appear here – even if brushed over. These then become huge issues as we begin to execute

– issues around team harmony, engagement, and ultimately quality and outcome.

A better way to handle this is to create the *structure* of the stance you want to take, and leave room for change in the *content* that goes into the structure. Let me give you an example:

If your vision is to improve the way your customers interact with you for support, then your *structure* could be around the improvement of the customer satisfaction metrics: a decrease in complaints; an increase in sales. You should be unflagging around this structure. What should be open for creative collaboration is the *content* that goes into the structure – don't make up your mind that using a social media channel is the best way to improve customer support; don't make up your mind about the 10 steps that need to happen differently in the current process. If you go in with these pre-conceived notions around the content of the execution, you leave no room for collaboration. And if you don't have engagement at this stage, at best you will achieve mediocre results, and at worst you will fail in realizing the promised outcomes of the idea/vision.

The next time you move into "design" from "idea," check your *structure* and *content*. Be unflagging in the former and flexible in the latter.

Exercise # 7

COLLABORATING FOR EXECUTION – WHEN TO HOLD & WHEN TO FOLD

1. The next time you want to sell your idea or vision or a new approach, first write down what outcome you really want and then how you would measure your idea's success:

OUTCOMES:

_____

_____

_____

_____

_____

MEASURES OF SUCCESS:

_____

_____

_____

_____

_____

2. Then, list at least 3 ways you will define the idea and ask for collaboration around how to execute, instead of just giving your team/peer the actual steps (as you see them!):

_____

_____

_____

_____

_____

WHAT'S THE MAIN IDEA?

Most of us get stuck in a mode of "it isn't ready yet." I have seen so many folks struggle to get over the finish line – that last mile, as it were. Something holds us back – some feeling of "what if?" It is safer to be in the process than to face the results of our actions. What if we fail? What if the projections don't meet the outcomes? What if we are humiliated?

But the art of finishing is to get to 80% and deliver value at that crucial juncture.

8

GETTING TO 80% –
THE ART OF FINISHING

Finishing is important. We know starting is tough – to get off the couch takes a pretty significant effort. What is sometimes hidden is the fact that we fail to launch – even if we get off the couch. Regardless of your endeavor, simply polishing that diamond is not enough. For it to glow and shine, it has to be unwrapped! Projects must be completed – initiatives must be launched. Your personal and professional dreams must be converted into action that actually crosses a finish line.

Most of us get stuck in a mode of "it isn't ready yet." I have seen so many folks struggle to get over the finish line – that last mile, as it were. Something holds us back – some feeling of "what if?" It is safer to be in the process than to face the results of our actions. What if we fail? What if the projections don't meet the outcomes? What if we are humiliated?

There are some telltale signs that all of us can identify when the finish line is approaching, and sometimes past us! I don't want to sound trite, but the "80/20 rule," which is bandied about, actually does make sense. How do you know when you are at 80? How do you wrap it up and take that final leap? Here are some rules of thumb I use, and I hope they help you as well:

1. Your (or team's) intensity of effort is high, but the *increments* in outcomes are falling rapidly.

2. "Finishing touches" are taking >80% of your effort on a consistent basis.

3. Your baseline milestones are being met (or have been met) – but you are now creating additional ones. (Additional improvements are fine – but why can't they wait for the next "version" of your initiative?)

4. You have checked off all the "to-dos," but have a hollow feeling in your stomach. Trust me – this feeling is telling you to launch! It's the same feeling you get when you are about to jump off a plane/step off to do a bungee jump!!!!!

5. You are finding all the ways things could go wrong, instead of the fewer things that could and will go right.

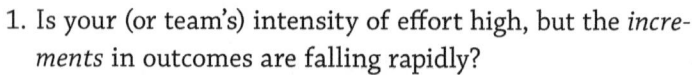

Exercise # 8

GETTING TO 80% - THE ART OF FINISHING

1. Is your (or team's) intensity of effort high, but the *increments* in outcomes are falling rapidly?

No	Maybe	Yes, Definitely
○	○	○
(Score = 1)	(Score = 3)	(Score = 5)

2. Are "Finishing touches" taking >80% of your effort on a consistent basis?

No	Maybe	Yes, Definitely
○	○	○
(Score = 1)	(Score = 3)	(Score = 5)

3. Are your baseline milestones being met (or have been met) – but you are now creating additional ones? (Additional improvements are fine – but why can't they wait for the next "version" of your initiative?)

No	Maybe	Yes, Definitely
○	○	○
(Score = 1)	(Score = 3)	(Score = 5)

4. Have you checked off all the "to-dos," but have a hollow feeling in your stomach?

No	Maybe	Yes, Definitely
○	○	○
(Score = 1)	(Score = 3)	(Score = 5)

5. Are you finding all the ways things could go wrong, instead of the fewer things that could and will go right?

No	Maybe	Yes, Definitely
○	○	○
(Score = 1)	(Score = 3)	(Score = 5)

IF YOUR TOTAL SCORE IS BETWEEN 15 AND 25

you are definitely procrastinating! You are ready to launch, but are stalling. It is time for you to launch!

IF YOUR TOTAL SCORE IS BETWEEN 10 AND 15

you probably are ready – but could benefit slightly by applying the finishing touches you want. So, go ahead and apply them – just don't delay forever!

IF YOUR TOTAL SCORE IS BETWEEN 5 AND 10

you are almost there – but you probably should be focused on completing your final tasks and activities.

WHAT'S THE MAIN IDEA?

How does an effective leader react and respond to setbacks? Here are some daily practices that I have modeled on their behavior:

1. Budget discrete time for disappointment.

2. Go back to your Personal Mission Statement.

3. Rapidly accelerate.

4. Find and finish.

5. Finally, surround yourself with the right people.

9

COUNTERING SETBACKS – LEADERSHIP BEHAVIORS

All of us have had (and will continue to have) some professional setbacks – prospects breaking off at the last moment after a seemingly agreeable interaction, clients refusing to renew, etc. While these examples are very specific to my situation, we all face "setbacks" frequently as we strive to achieve our transformational goals. It may be in our personal or professional lives, but setbacks and obstacles are here to stay with us. How does an effective leader react and respond to setbacks? While I can't say that I am totally immune to the vagaries of rejection and setbacks, here are some daily practices I use that have helped me. Hope they help you too!

#1 - Budget discrete time for disappointment – While I believe in positive psychology, I don't really believe in ignoring reality. I acknowledge the sinking feeling I get in my stomach when negative events occur! I know that it will make me feel discouraged and disappointed. What I have taught (and am constantly teaching) myself is to put a discrete timeline in my mind and tell myself that I will stop ruminating over the event after that arbitrary limit. Where you set that limit is up to you. The sooner the better, obviously. But you'll get better at it as you practice this behavior.

#2 - Go back to your Personal Mission Statement – The personal mission statement is one of my centering tools, and I especially go back to it when I have setbacks. Do the "whys" still hold true? Am I doing what I am doing for the right reasons? Do they align with my personal and professional themes for the year/future? This exercise serves to firm up my spine and point me back in the direction I should head. Do you have a personal mission statement? (Refer to Leadership Secret # 1.)

#3 - Rapidly accelerate – I shift up my "MPH," my "magnificent performance horsepower" to a different gear and focus intensely on my activity plans. I have found that nothing accelerates outcomes better than positive action. The time after a setback is the second-best time to accelerate (the best being when you succeed, more about that in a future chapter), so focus on action more than ever before. It is quite common to have doubts, of course, especially after a setback, which is why it is important to have a framework for action. I prefer to practice a weekly leadership ritual that gives me a discrete foundation for action. What about you? (Refer to Leadership Secret # 2 for the weekly leadership ritual.)

#4 - Find and finish – I pick an outcome in a space that I have influence over (current project, personal project, personal life) and finish it! It is important to me at this point to gain the feeling of achievement and credibility I get by successfully getting to a notable outcome. This is also the time to go after that one activity you have been procrastinating about. The best way to build your core back up is based on achievement and credibility.

#5 - Finally, surround yourself with the right people – This is exactly the wrong time to hang around people who don't understand your goals and vision. Unfortunately, many of those whom you consider close may fall into this category. It is simply best not to solicit any feedback from folks who say things like, "Well, it was always going to be tough to do that," or "This is why I didn't try to do that – I could have if I wanted to," or the best one of them all – "I told you so!!!" Understand that you don't have to react to this unsolicited feedback. Practice the art of selective hearing! If you have followed the other daily leadership behaviors that I discuss in this book, you will have sought out the right type of company by now. It is very important to seek support from a group of people who are positively inclined and are striving toward transformation just as you are.

Exercise # 9

COUNTERING SETBACKS –
LEADERSHIP BEHAVIORS

1. Write down what distressed you most about the setback you experienced. Read it and acknowledge that it impacted you. Jot down a "finish" time to close the book on what you wrote – turn the page, if you will.

_____

_____

_____

_____

_____

2. Review your Personal Mission Statement and test it with the following:

Do the "whys" still hold true?

_____

_____

_____

Am I doing what I am doing for the right reasons?

_____

_____

_____

Do they align with my personal and professional themes for the year/future?

_____

_____

_____

3. If you are aligned in the step above, then ramp up your activities! Practice your daily and weekly rituals. I typically refocus and intensify my weekly leadership ritual:

DESIGN YOUR CORE:

Are you performing activities that will take you further in accomplishing your personal mission?

_____

_____

_____

_____

FIRE IT UP:

Which one skill/technique will you add to your repertoire this week?

_____

_____

_____

_____

ACHIEVE CREDIBILITY:

What will you accomplish (finish) this week that will utilize your unique competencies?

_____

_____

_____

NURTURE & TRANSFORM:

Have you decided how you will help one other person in your sphere of influence to achieve their goals this week?

_____

_____

_____

WHAT'S THE MAIN IDEA?

What is holding you back in your career? What are some of the key levers effective leaders use to launch their careers into the stratosphere? There are two key levers:

1. They stopped worshipping at the altar of public opinion long ago.

2. They don't let the past limit them.

10

TWO LEVERS FOR SPECTACULAR CAREERS

Outstanding leaders always seem to find a way to thrive in their careers. Even if they seem to launch into non-traditional and alternative paths, they always seem to have their own targets in mind. How do they do this? What tools and techniques do they use as multipliers? They use two spectacular levers. Here they are:

Strategy # 1
Stop worshipping at the altar
of public opinion

Constantly designing and measuring yourself against milestones driven by others is a definite recipe for disaster. "Well, my title is the only way I can prove that I am valuable to others," "What will people think if I take this job/company; no one will really understand what I do – even though it will be something I know I am passionate about." I recently worked with someone who couldn't get out of a bad work situation, even though he had an opportunity to move to what seemed to meet all of his criteria except – the "title"! So he sacrificed the opportunity and stayed miserable, for the cost of what his social circle would think of him. We need the courage to accept that each of us is unique and is driven by certain passions and persuasions. Unless we design our milestones to match them, we are doomed to mediocrity. A personal mission statement helps! Use it to drive your path, not public opinion. (And yes, the number of "Likes" you get on Facebook has nothing to do with your ongoing fulfillment!!!)

Strategy # 2
Don't let the past be limiting

Frequently, I see (even well-meaning) bosses tell their subordinates, "Well, I don't think you are ready for that yet," or "I think based on what you have done so far, it won't be suitable for you." Personal and social well-wishers (or not) tend to throw a lot of FUD factor ("Fear, Uncertainty & Doubt") as well. "Are you sure you know what you are doing? I have never seen you do that before," or "What makes you think you can do that – you have no_____." The past is only a constraint to what others perceive about you! It has nothing at all to do with what you can aim, know and do – today and tomorrow. I use these phrases to align: Know Why; Know What; Know How and Do Now. It's nothing at all to do with the past –simply drive down your path based on your personal mission.

Exercise # 10

TWO LEVERS FOR SPECTACULAR CAREERS

1. As you embark on defining the next step in your career, first answer these questions:

Know Why – Why is this next step important to you? Why is it a reflection of your Core and how does it map to your personal mission statement?

_____

_____

_____

_____

_____

_____

Know What – Can you define what you want to achieve in your career? Is it specific, measurable, attainable, results-based and timely?

_____

_____

_____

_____

_____

_____

Know How – Do you have a plan? What are the discrete monthly, weekly and daily activities you are going to perform to create a spectacular career?

_____

_____

_____

_____

_____

_____

2. If you have worked through the questions above, what are you waiting for? Do Now – get started and work the plan you created. As you immerse yourself, notice that getting stuck in the past or on public opinion is not part of the plan!

WHAT'S THE MAIN IDEA?

Are you holding back? Why? WHY? You are the most precious asset you can give to an initiative – if you hold back, then you are shortchanging everyone, including yourself. Jump out!

11

ARE YOU HOLDING YOURSELF BACK?

During a particularly difficult time professionally, someone I respect and admire a lot stopped me in my tracks when he asked me, "Why are you holding yourself back?" I was shocked! Holding back? Me??!! Ridiculous, I thought. (This was in conjunction with a business idea he wanted me to collaborate on.) I took this as a personal affront. But when I reflected, I knew this person only wished me well; he had nothing to gain by being untruthful or hurtful to me. I reflected some more – by withdrawing totally from gainful work (I don't necessarily recommend this for everyone – but it works for me!) and pushing the "pause" button to re-evaluate. I asked myself:

When I entered into a commitment, was I plunging into it with the fullest intensity of my mind and body? Or was I holding just that last bit back, in case I failed? In case "it" failed? In case I lost all my money? In case I became penniless, jobless, business-less, in case...in case....in case....If I'm not all in, why not? WHY NOT?

The sabbatical helped refocus me. I got back at it – I did something that was completely new to me and I decided to jump from the plane without a parachute. I bet that my belief and conviction would reach out and hook me before I hit the ground!

Are you holding back? Why? WHY? You are the most precious asset you can give to an initiative – if you hold back, then you are shortchanging everyone, including yourself. Jump out!

Exercise # 11

ARE YOU HOLDING YOURSELF BACK?

Here is a checklist that will help you to figure out whether you are holding yourself back. If you are checking more than 3 in this list, you need to change your state. Stop doing these things and you will find yourself on your way.

1. Didn't (or won't) start stuff.

2. No personal measure of success – always comparing to others' definitions of success.

3. Lots of hand wringing – not enough hand raising.

4. The finger is always pointing outward, never inward!

5. Blaming a "lack of talent" – or the other side of the coin – explaining others' success with the "well, he is really talented at that....." – no worth or weight given to the mission, relentless practice and achievement shown by them.

6. Confusing power with abuse.

7. Wondering what happened instead of making something happen.

8. Won't ever forgive self.

9. Thinking small, when BIG is right around the corner.

10. Forgetting that grand plans always boil down to daily rituals.

WHAT'S THE MAIN IDEA?

If you look at successful people, you will find that they take control of "their stories." While external events always influence what we do, it is up to us to define our own stories. It is the difference in how ultra-effective leaders are able to show conviction during the most hopeless of times and drive themselves and their teams to achieve fulfillment.

12

WHAT'S YOUR STORY?

Sometimes we let negative experiences drive our behavior and life for far too long. In essence, it becomes the "story of our life" for that period of time. Now, these "negative" experiences may be real or perceived, large or small, personal or professional, but a common thread is that they disrupt out flow and push us off center.

I once had a client who had worked hard to reach a middle management position at a large organization. She was well liked by her team and got along with her colleagues. She did, however, work for a manipulative boss who sacrificed her to further his own career. She was sidelined and made into an "also-ran." She never recovered from what she perceived as a death knell to her career and remained stuck for years. Essentially, she made that one event, significant as it was, her "story." She was forever lamenting the "unfairness" of it all to whoever would listen, and made no effort either to change herself or her environment. She seemed to have hit a wall and just couldn't get up. In short, she exhibited these classic behaviors:

1. Didn't (or won't) start stuff.

2. Lots of hand wringing – not enough hand raising.

3. The finger is always pointing outward, never inward!

4. Wondering what happened instead of making something happen.

5. Won't ever forgive self.

6. Thinking small, when BIG is right around the corner.

If you look at successful people, you will find that they take control of "their stories." While external events always influence what we do, it is up to us to define our own stories. It is the difference in how ultra-effective leaders are able to show conviction during the most hopeless of times and drive themselves and their teams to achieve fulfillment. So how do they avoid the trap of letting others define their stories? Exercise # 12 provides a quick checklist for you to follow while staying on track with your own story.

Exercise # 12

WHAT'S YOUR STORY?

1. Escape the trap by practicing the following leadership behaviors:

   a. Don't view shortcuts as the kiss of death.

   b. Acknowledge obstacles as temporary roadblocks and not as initiative-ending events.

   c. Use language like "what can be done"/"alternatively, we could do ___"/"that could be in Phase 2"/"I may know of a way to get around that."

   d. Focus more on outcomes of activities and less on the inputs and outputs.

   e. Simplify communication as the stress increases and focus less on jargon and obfuscation.

   f. Expect to be evaluated based on contributions and outcomes, rather than on "your place in the universe."

   g. Increasingly ignore hierarchical bluster and gatekeeping.

   h. "Call teammates and partners out" to pull their weight if it is not happening.

    i. Skip the "established lines of communication" to prise out issues and smooth over and manage expectations.

    j. Don't indulge in hand wringing.

    k. Focus on daily progress, almost to the exclusion of the "big picture."

    l. Focus more on value in terms of tangible outcomes and less on "What I am supposed to do?"

2. Some of the earlier exercises in this book will help you keep your story on track:

    a. Exercise # 1 – Your Personal Mission Statement

    b. Exercise # 9 – Countering setbacks – Leadership behaviors (Weekly Leadership Ritual)

    c. Exercise # 2 – Build Your Leadership Launch Platform

WHAT'S THE MAIN IDEA?

Whenever anyone says something is "hand-crafted" it conjures up visions of artistic beauty, intricate detail and unique perspectives. How can an effective leader "handcraft" her leadership behaviors as she leads herself and her teams towards exceptional performance and fulfillment? Four traits borrowed from handcrafting:

1. Passion

2. Fierce Focus

3. The Small Things

4. Ownership

13

HANDCRAFTING YOUR LEADERSHIP BEHAVIOR

Feeling rushed, under pressure to produce, pushes us to just tick off the things we need to do every day. At risk, of course, is the *how* we do these things. If we are defined at work by what we produce and how we influence other people (which we are), then how can we not perform our daily activities like craftsmen? How can we not handcraft our leadership behaviors? Our behaviors cannot be "canned" and resemble the output of an assembly line. To move yourself and your team to achieve exceptional outcomes, will a cookie cutter approach suffice? Or do you need to handcraft your behavior every day? I would vote for the latter. Let's borrow four traits of handcrafting and apply them to leadership behavior:

1. **Passion** – Be passionate about pushing forward to achieving a larger outcome. That doesn't mean that all of us are trying to save the world (although, why not?) – it does mean, however, that you have a

larger collaborative outcome in mind, and are able to convey that passion – both to yourself and your team.

2. **Fierce Focus** – This may manifest as attention to detail sometimes, extreme intensity to finish at other times, but is always focused on the outcome at hand and how you can enable your teams to achieve it – at all times – exclusively.

3. **The Small Things** – Do the small things well – the nurturing that needs to happen every day with your team. The empathy you need to show and the relationships you have to build. The Small Things have a Big Payoff.

4. **Ownership** – Give all of yourself – don't hold back. If you are constantly looking over your shoulder, or worried about the safety net, you will miss the boat.

Exercise # 13

HANDCRAFTING YOUR LEADERSHIP BEHAVIOR

1. Review your weekly action plan. Look at all the activities you have planned. Do you think they will lead to a sum that is greater than the individual parts? (i.e., do you think they will help you execute your personal mission statement?) If yes – write why. If no, write why not and how you can steer your week back.

_____

_____

_____

_____

_____

2. Ask your team members (you can do this informally in a team meeting – show of hands is good enough) to rate how focused they are on the outcomes of the project all of you are involved in. Do they understand what the outcome is? Are they focused on it or are they concerned about completing tasks?

Fiercely focused . . . . ( )

Focused on the outcome most of the time . . . . ( )

Focused on the outcome some of the time . . . . ( )

Just want to get my tasks done . . . . ( )

Get to the bottom of why fierce focus is an issue. Realign back to the original.

3. Do you find your team spending a disproportionate amount of time on "vision" and "strategy"? (Assuming you have been asked to execute to a given set of strategies). Is your team's "hat too big for its cattle?" (!!!!) i.e., is it all talk of big things and not enough concern about executing the details? If so, start to get them focused on milestones and deliverables and convince them that "vision" and "strategy" find physical manifestation in the dirt and noise of execution.

4. First, do this exercise on your own behavior. Next, ask your teammates to join in and share their results:

   a. Evaluate your behavior in the past week during meetings, interactions with peers, bosses and customers, phone calls, emails, etc. Be honest!

   (i) Did you find yourself getting stuck to the mechanics of an idea rather than the spirit of it?

   _____

   _____

   _____

   If so, then ask yourself whether you want to see your idea in action (i.e., being executed) or sacrifice the general "structure" of it because you couldn't let the idea be fully baked with other opinions and "content." The key here is to be fully committed to your idea, of course – but to the structure of it rather than all the exact details. You will find that if you can get others to fill in your idea, you will have team commitment – although you will have to live with the fact that the idea may look and feel different from what you had envisioned.

(ii) Did you find yourself trying to "protect" an existing system/process/"way of doing things" simply because you were involved in its origination?

_____

_____

_____

If so, let go! This is never a good reason for getting stuck. To make forward progress, you have to let go of this safety tether, however difficult it is for you.

(iii) Did you find yourself agreeing to a decision half-heartedly, thinking that you could always excuse your lack of cooperation later to not having fully agreed?

_____

_____

_____

Here is the golden rule – keep your disagreements and consensus building inside the protected atmosphere of your team. Disagreement, arguments and eventual consensus are absolutely healthy for a high-performance team. What is unhealthy and downright dysfunctional is to somehow think that you retain a right to derail team decisions once they are "made" within the team.

WHAT'S THE MAIN IDEA?

Henry Ford failed multiple times before he established the Ford Motor Company. Even after establishing his company, success came late.

Akio Morita's first product was a rice cooker that was a whopping failure. Reportedly, he sold only 100 units! If his name is not familiar – he is the founder of Sony.

Michael Jordan, the iconic basketball star, says it best: "I have missed more than 9,000 shots in my career. I have lost almost 300 games. On 26 occasions I have been entrusted to take the game-winning shot, and I missed. I have failed over and over and over again in my life. And that is why I succeed."

14

HOW GOOD IS YOUR "SECOND SERVE"?

When a tennis player attempts a second serve, she has two choices. The first option is to de-risk it completely by "spinning it in." This option, while safe and with a high probability that the ball will be in play, also takes away the one big advantage a server has – the serve is supposed to be an offensive weapon, setting you up to succeed and win, not a defensive or "safe" tactic to use to "stay in the game." In fact, coaches at the junior level are always telling their ward to "swing faster" on their second serves – not to decrease intensity, but to just change the angle of the swing to increase the safety factor. So that is the second option – swing faster, but at a different angle.

Frequently, we are in the situation of getting ready for the "second serve" in business and in life. How offensive (i.e., results-oriented) it is will determine (a) whether you stick to your endeavor and (b) whether the outcome will match your vision. All of us have the tendency to "wait" for certain events, things, etc., to happen before we will take that "fast swing." I hear this many times: "Once this important project is finished, I will get that training and certification that will put me at the next level," or "Once he gets back from vacation, I will discuss the unprofessional attitude of my boss toward my team," or "I think if I become 'Director' (or plug in your favorite tile here...) then I can really show 'leadership.'" It is like we took that first serve when we joined a new job/endeavor/project. Let's say it was a bit lukewarm, and suddenly we feel we need to wait and be safe before we can launch. Swinging faster on that second serve requires a few important attributes:

- Relentless practice of your skills in all scenarios – it is not sufficient to exhibit your strengths (maybe you have always been told "you are a great communicator," or "you really know how to calm agitated people down and get them to focus," or "we can always come to you when this customer gets frantic," when times are good – but you have to be able to leverage your core strengths even when things get frantic. That is a true indicator of how valuable you are to your organization and, in turn, how fulfilled you will be at the workplace. Your "second serve" will become more reliable as you stay true to your Core, even in crises.

- A complete abandonment of the stain of the past. I have never met a hyper-successful, fulfilled individual who dwells on how the past is constraining him. Super-successful leaders always believe that the future is spotless. This allows them to "swing faster" on that important second serve! Some famous examples:

- Henry Ford failed multiple times before he established the Ford Motor Company. Even after establishing his company, success came late.

- Akio Morita's first product was a rice cooker that was a whopping failure. Reportedly, he sold only 100 units! If his name is not familiar – he is the founder of Sony.

- Michael Jordan, the iconic basketball star, says it best: "I have missed more than 9,000 shots in my career. I have lost almost 300 games. On 26 occasions I have been entrusted to take the game-winning shot, and I missed. I have failed over and over and over again in my life. And that is why I succeed."

History is littered with people who swung faster on their second serve. How aggressive is your second serve?

Exercise # 14

HOW GOOD IS YOUR "SECOND SERVE"?

1. First, make sure you have completed Exercise # 1. It is extremely important you figure out your Core first.

_____ Yes; _____ No (Then what are you waiting for? Go complete Exercise # 1!!!)

2. Review your behavior over the past month at work. Grade yourself: (Circle the grade you think you should get.)

1. When things didn't go as planned, how likely were you to rely on your strengths and intensify your efforts?

Not Likely	Somewhat Likely	Likely	Very Likely
◯	◯	◯	◯
1	2	3	4

2. When primary plans fail (or are abandoned), how likely is it that your peers/bosses come to you for guidance?

Not Likely	Somewhat Likely	Likely	Very Likely
◯	◯	◯	◯
1	2	3	4

3. Do you find yourself "pulling back" and resorting to "safe" behaviors when project activity gets risky and people start pushing for direction and guidance?

Not Likely	Somewhat Likely	Likely	Very Likely
◯	◯	◯	◯
4	3	2	1

4. Do you find yourself "passed over" when "war room" (i.e., crisis/critical issue) projects have to be completed?

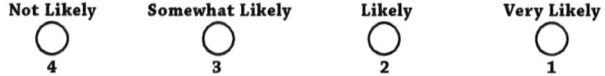

Not Likely	Somewhat Likely	Likely	Very Likely
4	3	2	1

3. Add your individual grades. What is your total? Here is a handy guide to help you work on your "second serve" behaviors. Remember, this is not a one-time exercise – you must come back to this and grade yourself periodically to ensure you stay on the right track.

SCORE BETWEEN 12 AND 16
You are doing great. Keep swinging!

SCORE BETWEEN 8 AND 12
You sometimes worry about pushing faster and harder when "Plan B" takes effect. Examine your behaviors and start to leverage and depend on your core strengths, even during frantic times.

SCORE BETWEEN 4 AND 8
You are playing it safe! This may be inhibiting your progress. More importantly, it is definitely stopping you from climbing the leadership ascent curve. And ultimately, it is stopping you from finding fulfillment at work. So, go back and re-evaluate your personal mission statement in Exercise # 1. Then begin to abandon the fear tied to failure and start focusing on leadership behaviors that will move you steadily away from the fear of the past toward the promise of the future. Remember – your future is spotless at any given time!

WHAT'S THE MAIN IDEA?

Daniel Pink, in *Drive*, talks about the "operating system" for motivation and the fact that it is outdated to fit today's workplace. Leadership requires its own operating system. I believe that the type of leader you are, the intensity of followership you are blessed with and the breadth of impact you have are all related to your Core.

15

HAVE YOU CHECKED ON THE HEALTH OF YOUR OPERATING SYSTEM LATELY?

We are all updating our smartphones, our computers, and our "clouds" with the latest version of whatever operating system that runs these devices. Some of us wouldn't be caught dead with an older version of software! It is almost a  black mark on our reputations as device-toting professionals of the modern era. But what about the "software" that drives us – as human beings, as professionals in the workplace and ultimately, as travelers looking for fulfillment?

Daniel Pink, in *Drive*, talks about the "operating system" for motivation and the fact that it is outdated to fit today's workplace. Leadership requires its own operating system. I believe that the type of leader you are, the intensity of followership you are blessed with and the breadth of impact you have are all related to your Core. As in, what is your Core? How do your competencies drive your daily leadership behavior? How have you designed your unique contribution to your team, your organization and your community?

Tom works for a large healthcare company. He had reached a senior managerial level at his organization based on past achievements. However, he felt stuck. He thought it was potently unfair that seemingly less experienced people than him were getting more visibility and rewards. He was upset with his boss Nancy, and this reflected on his behavior toward his own team as well. He thought he had been an excellent leader and just couldn't understand how he wasn't being rewarded. He sat down with Nancy and told her directly that he felt that he was being sidelined. Nancy, who was an excellent leader herself smiled and said, "I have been waiting for you to have this chat. I would have brought it up in the near future – but I wanted you to feel the urgency yourself." Tom was perplexed. Why would Nancy delay this important discussion? And Nancy surprised him further by asking him to meet with some of his own team to gather their feedback before she would give him any direction. Tom, frustrated and a bit angry, decided to talk to his senior most team member John, who had been with Tom since they started their careers more than two decades ago. John was a steady and reliable contributor, usually the rock of any team. He wasn't interested in traditional corporate ladder climbing and kept well away from territorial politics. He was, however, an impact player as he had built deep product expertise as well as longstanding customer relationships. John smiled at Tom and said, "Well, I am glad we are talking about this because I have been concerned about you. Lately you have been very short with your team and it is not like you at all." He continued, "Tom, have you looked at your team composition lately?" Tom replied, "What do you mean? The number of people?" John said, "No, look at the average age of your team – they are younger by ten years now than even a couple of years ago." Tom reflected and said, "Yes, you are probably right. I never paid any attention to that." John looked at Tom for a minute and asked him, "Do you think the skills you use to motivate me and folks my age and experience work with your younger team members? Have you taken the time and effort to reskill yourself and understand what drives them so you can lead them better?" Tom was taken aback. Had he lost his skills? John said, "Tom, you are still a good leader and a great person to work with. You just don't connect with your team anymore. And Nancy and the other seniors have noticed that. Our performance has slipped a bit and we have missed a couple of deadlines in the past six months. The team doesn't respond to authoritative directives anymore – you have to earn their trust and build consensus." Tom was beginning to understand. "I understand what you are saying, but this is how my leaders led me, and this is what has worked for me. If I am to change, I really need help." John helpfully replied, "You know that HR actually has a 'New Generation Leadership' program that I have heard a lot about. And they even have an ongoing coaching program that I am sure Nancy will enroll you in. I think that would help a lot." Tom ruefully thanked John and hurried into Nancy's office and barged in. Nancy looked at him and said, "Tom, what's the matter? You look pumped!" Tom said, "Nancy, I figured it out. I need to polish up my core skills. They have tarnished a bit!" Nancy smiled and said, "Okay, Tom sit down. Now let's have that chat and then we can figure out how to put you back on track."

You can see that Tom had to re-evaluate his "operating system" and "upgrade" it! He had to refresh it to keep him relevant. By doing so, it helped him get back on track and resume his leadership journey.

Exercise # 15

HAVE YOU CHECKED ON THE HEALTH OF YOUR OPERATING SYSTEM LATELY?

Is your Operating System Open Source or Commercial? (Are you in this for purely monetary rewards or a longer-term, sustainable objective?) Listen, be honest – both models obviously work in the computer industry.

_____

_____

_____

_____

_____

Does your Operating System perform fast and reliably under peak loads? (Do you have a core set of competencies that you rely on to execute at exceptional levels, especially under pressure?)

_____

_____

_____

_____

_____

Does your Operating System support a large number of applications? (Do you know how to enable, rather than direct and control? Do you know how to play well with others?)

_____

_____

_____

_____

Does your Operating System try to occupy a lot of space and features and try to gobble up single-feature tools? (Are you able to rely on your peers/teams/bosses and trust them to perform their roles as you perform yours? Or do you have to do it all and always be at the forefront?)

_____

_____

_____

_____

Can your Operating System be upgraded smoothly, with a minimum amount of loss to existing features and capabilities? (Do you have the capacity to continue refreshing your Core, learning new skills, while retaining an unflagging Core?

_____

_____

_____

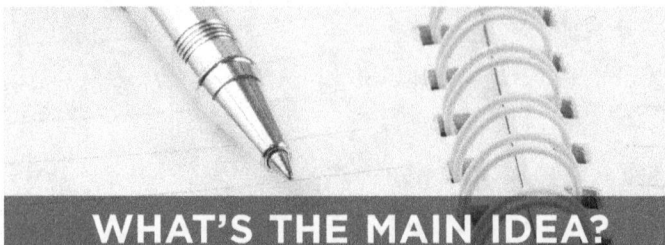

WHAT'S THE MAIN IDEA?

Why is there such a fuss over who has what title? As far as titles being tied to reward (compensation), while that may be part of the reason, I am not convinced that it is a good enough reason to sully your days at work with an obsession about hierarchies and titles. Because you know what? I believe that there is an innate and implicit hierarchy anyway. And this hierarchy is based on capability, credibility and influence.

16

STOP LOOKING AT THAT ORG CHART!

At a large multi-billion-dollar organization I consulted for, I saw an amazing phenomenon daily. Every day, employees of the division I was advising would arrive at work, login to their computers… and the first thing they did was to check the company's org chart application, which was available to them on their Intranet. They checked on who moved up, sideways and down, and what their past and current titles were. Suffice it to say that no one found themselves magically promoted without their own knowledge! And of course, the inevitable grumbling and complaining of how unworthy the few who got promoted were, took over the early morning social conversations. What a terrible way to start the day!

Why is there such a fuss over who has what title? As far as titles being tied to reward (compensation), while that may be part of the reason, I am not convinced that it is a good enough reason to sully your days at work with an obsession about hierarchies and titles. Because you know what? I believe that there is an innate and implicit hierarchy anyway. And this hierarchy is based on capability, credibility and influence. Let me explain with a story:

My son is an elite level junior tennis player. Most days of the week, after school, you will find him practicing with a group of peers under the watchful eyes of his club coaches. Recently, I watched one of those practices. After the initial warm-up drills, the head coach gathered the kids around him, went through the particular skills he wanted to emphasize for that day, and then began assigning players to courts.

The way it works is, there is a "ladder" – an explicit hierarchy that is listed on a bulletin board – based on some complex calculation of points won and lost, games won and lost over an extended period, and frequently it is outdated and there are many errors in it. The kids hardly pay attention to that.

Then there is a hierarchy of courts as well. Court 1 goes to the best two players that day, Court 2 to the next best and so on. The best two players on any particular day are defined by who beat whom over the recent past – a more accurate reflection of the ladder. Well, this particular day, it so happened that my son got to play on Court 1 and the coach sent another kid to play against my son. My son immediately declared to the other kid, "I am taking this side and you take the other side" (the other side being the "bad" side, with the Texas sun beating down mercilessly, making serving difficult). While the other kid grumbled a bit (my son and he are very close in their tennis levels right now), he didn't complain. Just as he was about to go to the other side of the court, the coach intervened and said that he had made a mistake, and based on last week's results, my son actually needed to play a different kid. So, the original opponent walked away to a different court to be replaced by the new one – who happened to be the # 1 ranked kid in my son's age group. My son's opponent walked over to the "good" side of the court and motioned to my son to take the other side, which my son dutifully did without so much as a murmur.

The innate hierarchy was in play here! This was the hierarchy of excellence, of achievement and of credibility – not one borne out of a chart on a piece of paper or on a webpage. It was beautiful to watch, but at the same time made me wonder – why do we forget what kids seem to know implicitly? That credibility and accomplishment are outcomes of achievement – they cannot be manufactured in any other way.

Why can't we use the same barometer in our corporate lives? Maybe we should stop checking the org chart and start practicing our craft. Maybe it is time to stop worrying about the flimsy ladder of corporate hierarchy and start laying the foundation for that innate hierarchy of accomplishment.

Exercise # 16

STOP LOOKING AT THAT ORG CHART!

1. List 5 instances in the recent past where you have either (a) not done something you knew should be done because "it wasn't in your job description" or (b) identified something in the team that you knew should be addressed, but decided that it was "above your pay grade."

i. _____

_____

ii. _____

_____

iii. _____

_____

iv. _____

_____

v. _____

_____

2. Identify 5 upcoming events/activities/issues where you will plan to avoid thinking about your title or position in the hierarchy and do what is right, based on your core competencies. Then list a set of discrete steps you will take to make this happen.

Identify Potential Events/ Activities/Issues	List Action Plan Items
1.	a. b. c. d.
2.	a. b. c. d.
3.	a. b. c. d.
4.	a. b. c. d.
5.	a. b. c. d.

WHAT'S THE MAIN IDEA?

As a leader, your chance at almost guaranteed success is to enable and nurture your teams – so putting arbitrary limits within which you "tolerate" performance will not generate the outcomes you are looking for. And as an individual and a personal leader, these will only serve to limit your ability to perform exceptional work, and ultimately stop short at finding fulfillment.

17

WHAT IS YOUR LEADERSHIP TOLERANCE LEVEL?

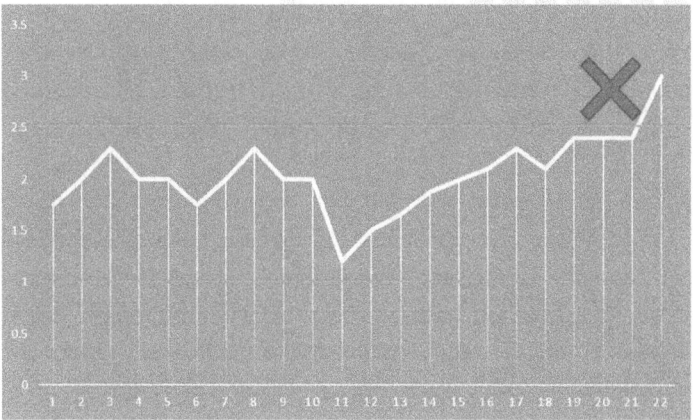

When I plied my trade as a mechanical engineer (seems like a past lifetime; nevertheless, good lessons were learnt there), I worked as a process engineer in one of my jobs. What this meant was that I stood for eight hours a day monitoring a process line that extruded copper and insulated the wire with plastic. I was monitoring the process so that neither the thickness of the copper nor the layers of insulation went beyond what engineers refer to as "tolerance limits." For example, in the sample chart in this blog – the lower limit is 1 unit and the upper limit is 2.5 units of measure. So, as long as the process stays within these limits of "tolerance," we allow it to continue humming; if it spikes either above or below (for whatever reason), we intervene, find, fix and reset. It is all mostly automated –so after a teething duration, intervention is not called for, unless there are extreme shifts.

What does this have to do with human leadership, you say? Whether you are a manager, senior leader or an individual who is a personal leader – are you setting limits to your leadership? If you are a leader who is responsible for other people's performance, do you try to keep them within some boundaries; and if they trend upwards, is your tolerance limit broken? That is, do you steer them back to the status quo with admonitions like, "Well, we cannot step on their toes," or "Unfortunately, that is not our resource and therefore we cannot drive it," etc., etc.? Wait! It cuts both ways. As an individual, do you wait for others to develop your career? Do you depend completely on your organization or your supervisor to provide you the beacons for your leadership journey?

Well, if you do – then you are in the "intolerance zone" on your leadership journey. It may work well when you want to ensure the highest quality of wires, but it won't work when you are trying to improve human performance. As a leader, your chance at almost guaranteed success is to enable and nurture your teams – so putting arbitrary limits within which you "tolerate" performance will not generate the outcomes you are looking for. And as an individual and a personal leader, these will only serve to limit your ability to perform exceptional work, and ultimately stop short at finding fulfillment.

So, shed those limits and break out of that intolerance zone! We have no alternative if we wish to lead excellent lives and find fulfillment.

Exercise # 17

WHAT IS YOUR LEADERSHIP TOLERANCE LEVEL?

1. First, make sure you have completed Exercise # 1. It is extremely important that you first figure out your Core.

_____ Yes;

_____ No (Then what are you waiting for? Go complete Exercise # 1!!!)

2. Review your behavior over the past month at work. Grade yourself (Circle the grade you think you should get):

1. Do you give yourself reasons not to push beyond acceptable levels of performance due to title, past experience, organizational politics, etc.?

Not Likely	Somewhat Likely	Likely	Very Likely
○	○	○	○
4	3	2	1

2. Do you catch yourself admonishing your team members to "just do our jobs, and not worry about the other stuff," or "We need to stay within our bounds," etc.?

Not Likely	Somewhat Likely	Likely	Very Likely
○	○	○	○
4	3	2	1

3. Do you feel that you "hold" yourself or your team back when you know your skills and expertise could help the situation?

Not Likely	Somewhat Likely	Likely	Very Likely
○	○	○	○
4	3	2	1

4. Are you likely to shut down your team members' ideas if you feel that they would disrupt organizational dynamics?

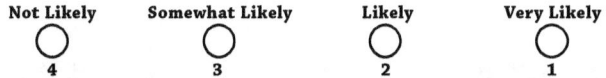

Not Likely	Somewhat Likely	Likely	Very Likely
◯	◯	◯	◯
4	3	2	1

3. Add your individual grades. What is your total? Here is a handy guide to help you work on your leadership tolerance levels. Remember, this is not a one-time exercise – you must come back to this and grade yourself periodically to ensure you stay on the right track.

SCORE BETWEEN 12 AND 16

You are doing great. You are not using artificial limits to constrain your leadership behavior. Continue to push beyond the limits actively.

SCORE BETWEEN 8 AND 12

You sometimes worry about organizational boundaries, titles and territorial politics. Examine your behaviors and start to push higher, even during frantic times.

SCORE BETWEEN 4 AND 8

You are safely within whatever limits you/your organization/your team have put on yourself. Whether they are realistic or artificial, you seem to stay in this "safe" zone. This may be inhibiting your progress. More importantly, it is definitely stopping you from climbing the leadership ascent curve. And ultimately, it is stopping you from finding fulfillment at work. So, go back and re-evaluate your personal mission statement in Exercise # 1. Then begin to abandon the fear tied to failure and start focusing on leadership behaviors that will move you steadily away from the fear of the past toward the promise of the future. Remember – your future is spotless at any given time!

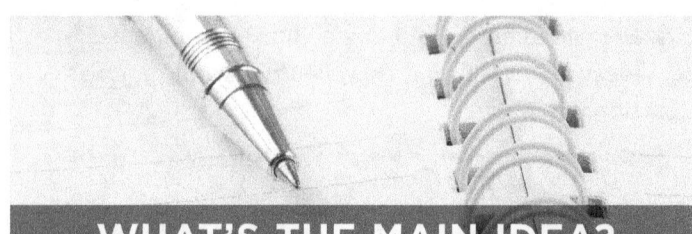

WHAT'S THE MAIN IDEA?

How can you aim for exceptional performance if you are neither passionate nor purposeful in your work? And, ultimately – how can you be relevant and fulfill yourself?

I say – give yourself permission to be passionate at work! If you believe in the purpose, go ahead and wear it on your sleeve. Then, watch the magic that follows.

18

LEADING WITH PASSION, PURPOSE & WITHOUT COMPROMISE

When I lead initiatives, I get passionate about their purpose. Earlier on in my career, I thought "passion" was a disadvantage. I was sometimes told that I was being too "emotional" about certain issues, that it was really not possible for others to focus on the "objective" stuff when I was being "passionate."

What nonsense!

If you are spending 40+ hours at work in a week and you are not passionate about its purpose, then you are short-changing yourself. What, are you going to delay that part of you till you "leave" work? Is it like a switch you suddenly turn on? Even if you could, which is highly questionable, what a tremendous waste of time to execute work in a dispassionate, unfulfilled way!

How can you aim for exceptional performance if you are

neither passionate nor purposeful in your work? And, ultimately – how can you be relevant and fulfill yourself?

I say – give yourself permission to be passionate at work! If you believe in the purpose, go ahead and wear it on your sleeve. Then, watch the magic that follows.

To sustain my passion and purpose, I leverage two key lessons my parents taught me early on. I call them the "2 Cs" of leadership.

My mother always said, "It doesn't matter what you do, where you are and how high you go – always take care of your Character (yes, with a capital "C"). A spot on your character spells your doom." That's how she raised us.

I remember attending my father's retirement speech – a consistent theme – (no) Compromise. He spoke about how he had navigated his entire career with no compromises. He told stories about how that probably closed some doors, but how it opened others. But also, how ultimately that led to the most fulfilling version of a career he could have carved out for himself.

How am I doing in the 2 Cs? I would give myself an A on Character – if you asked the people around me, there would be no questions around my faith, loyalty and honesty.

I would give myself a B on (no) Compromise. Actually, it might have been lower a few years ago – but I am working hard to correct that and pull myself back to an A! I could give many excuses – but this is really an issue of will and persistence. My goal is still to score an A.

How do you score on the 2 Cs? Food for thought...

Exercise # 18

LEADING WITH PASSION, PURPOSE & WITHOUT COMPROMISE

1. List 3 drivers that come to your mind when you ask yourself: "Why do I go to work?"

i. _____

ii. _____

iii. _____

2. Are you passionate about these 3 drivers? Can you identify the purpose behind them?

3 Top Drivers	Passion	Purpose
i.		
ii.		
iii.		

3. When you work toward accomplishing your top 3 drivers, rate your strength of character and your ability to hold your ground without compromise (5 being the strongest and 1 being the weakest).

3 Top Drivers	Strength of Character	Without Compromise
i.	◯ ◯ ◯ ◯ ◯ 1 2 3 4 5	◯ ◯ ◯ ◯ ◯ 1 2 3 4 5
ii.	◯ ◯ ◯ ◯ ◯ 1 2 3 4 5	◯ ◯ ◯ ◯ ◯ 1 2 3 4 5
iii.	◯ ◯ ◯ ◯ ◯ 1 2 3 4 5	◯ ◯ ◯ ◯ ◯ 1 2 3 4 5

WHAT'S THE MAIN IDEA?

Ultimately, what we must realize is that we work amongst human beings and not everything has to be viewed in terms of "beating" someone else to achieve your objectives. An effective leadership behavior, then, is to practice "transforming while enabling" – achieving your objectives by enabling others, not by beating them.

19

THE ZERO SUM GAME – OR IS IT?

We use sports metaphors in business and sometimes the win/win, win/lose lose/lose stuff gets pretty confusing. Do you have to "beat" someone to "win"?

How do you approach a situation that, seemingly at first blush, is a zero sum game (i.e., for you to achieve your objective, you have to "beat" someone)? Stephen Covey puts forth the "Win/Win or No Deal" model in his seminal classic, 7 *Habits of Highly Effective People*. To summarize – his model is that we need to move away from our internal scripting, which constantly tells us that to win, someone has to lose.

How do we take this "effective habit" and add it to our toolbox of daily leadership behavior?

I want to recount a personal experience here where I had to force myself into this model. I hope that this anecdote illustrates how we can practice this daily leadership behavior:

I was working with a junior executive at my client's organization to structure his operational processes. This junior executive, while receptive to my ideas, still had a lot of ownership with what he perceived to be his baby and was resisting some of the more impactful changes I was initiating. I had tried to orient him to my ideas, but he had resisted so far.

This is the quintessential example of the classic zero sum game – for me to push through my recommendations to my ultimate client (who happened to be the CEO of this company), I would have to "beat" this guy, right? But – this fellow was the key to actually executing the recommendations. Without his support, my recommendations would never leave the deck they graced, and my client wouldn't be served well at all.

My initial response was to assume an adversarial position with him, i.e., "have it out" with him to "close" the issue once and for all. I just happened to read the pertinent section of the Covey book the night before I was to meet with the junior executive to hash things out. The "Win/Win or No Deal" model really hit home, and I thought to myself that what I was planning to do was really not who I was – it was more of a conditioned, scripted response to a business situation. So, I rescripted myself and went about really understanding why this guy was resisting. His fears were that he didn't think his team was ready for the new operational processes and that "the way we did things around here" would break. I gently reminded him that things had already broken, and worse, they had customers really upset about the quality and cost of services being rendered to them. When I helped him peel the onion and presented my recommendations as enablers to his goals, he saw that he would win – not only the productivity and quality battle on his own turf, but more importantly, bring his customers back.

Ultimately, what we must realize is that we work amongst human beings and not everything has to be viewed in terms of "beating" someone else to achieve your objectives. An effective leadership behavior, then, is to practice "transforming while enabling" – achieving your objectives by enabling others, not by beating them.

Exercise # 19

THE ZERO SUM GAME – OR IS IT?

1. Review your behavior over the past month at work. Grade yourself (Circle the grade you think you should get):

1. Do you believe that for your idea/initiative to gain acceptance, you have to shut down other ideas/people?

Not Likely	Somewhat Likely	Likely	Very Likely
○	○	○	○
4	3	2	1

2. Do you find yourself focusing more on the cons of other ideas/people rather than on the pros of your own ideas?

Not Likely	Somewhat Likely	Likely	Very Likely
○	○	○	○
4	3	2	1

3. Do you react with an adversarial intent when you get pushback in meetings and legitimate discussions around ideas and recommendations?

Not Likely	Somewhat Likely	Likely	Very Likely
○	○	○	○
4	3	2	1

4. Are you able to isolate the merits and demerits of various ideas and recommendations from the personalities of the "messengers"?

Not Likely	Somewhat Likely	Likely	Very Likely
○	○	○	○
1	2	3	4

3. Add your individual grades. What is your total? Here is a handy guide to help you work on your leadership tolerance levels. Remember, this is not a one-time exercise – you must come back to this and grade yourself periodically to ensure you stay on the right track.

Score between 12 and 16

You are doing great. You are focused and objective about ideas. You have managed to stay away from mixing personalities with the merits of the ideas. You don't necessarily feel that you "win" or "lose" – just that there may be good or bad ideas. Keep your focus on staying objective and secure.

Score between 8 and 12

The heat of the battle gets to you sometimes! Just remember – you can "win" without having to beat somebody down – or you can gracefully concur with someone without having been "beaten."

Score between 4 and 8

You struggle with trying to isolate people from ideas and discussions. You strongly believe that you have to vanquish others to progress. Whether this is willful behavior or unintended is for you to evaluate. What is real, however, is that this mode of operation is definitely stopping you from climbing the leadership ascent curve. And ultimately, it is stopping you from finding fulfillment at work. As the workplace demographic evolves and people start to look at higher levels of human potential and fulfillment, the old ways of win/lose may not necessarily work for the best. Take an honest appraisal and work toward winning together. You do that by viewing and discussing ideas and initiatives dispassionately and impartially. In the long run, you will be leveraged as a true leader who can be depended upon even if you don't always "get your way." That is more rewarding than winning by rancor.

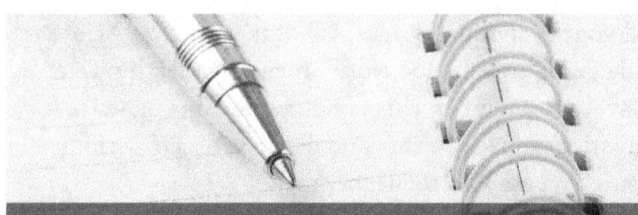

WHAT'S THE MAIN IDEA?

Fulfillment is driven by the impact you have. And impact is enabled by nurturing and enablement. How many people have you impacted? That is the Magic Number. Ultimately, where you are as a leader depends upon how and how many you have transformed.

20

WHAT IS YOUR MAGIC NUMBER?

And finally, my last (bonus) leadership secret for you. A magic number!

Pressure and practicalities tend to focus our efforts (and hence – our behaviors) on financial goals. The financial guys are always asking us, "What is your magic number to retire?" What if we focused on adding up our "magic number" like this?

- Number of people who trust you, and the number whom you trust.

- Number of people who depend on you, and on whom you depend upon.

- Number of people who can share uninhibitedly with you, and with whom you do the same.

Add these numbers. That is your Magic Number. I ran this exercise in a workshop with mid-level leaders at a large global firm. And initially, everyone complained, "Oh, but what if we don't deal with too many people in our jobs?" and, "But that's unfair! He is on the phone all the time and deals with a significant number of people!" etc., etc. So, should the focus be purely on the total number of people you can come up with who meet these criteria? Or are you satisfied with having fewer people, but with stronger relationships? You won't find the answer to that question here. That is for you to determine! All I can say is that there is no wrong answer and each one of us has to reconcile ourselves with the answer we come up with.

Exercise # 20

WHAT IS YOUR MAGIC NUMBER?

Answer the following questions from the perspective of your workplace. Don't limit yourself to your current job. Evaluate yourself and your experiences throughout your career. And if you want to use this as a barometer for your personal life, why – knock yourself out!

No.	Question	Score
1	How many people trust you?	
2	How many people do you trust?	
3	How many people depend on you?	
4	How many people do you depend on?	
5	How many people can you share important work issues with? (Not gossip!)	
6	How many people share important work issues with you?	
	TOTAL SCORE	

WHAT'S YOUR HEART TELLING YOU?

IN CONCLUSION –
LEADERSHIP ASCENT

Look at this chart. We are spending more time on work than on any other activity in our day. How, then, can we ignore the need to fulfill ourselves at work?

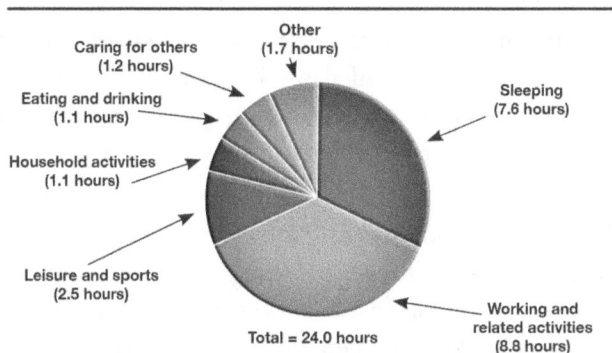

Time use on an average work day for employed persons ages 25 to 54 with children

Other
(1.7 hours)

Caring for others
(1.2 hours)

Eating and drinking
(1.1 hours)

Household activities
(1.1 hours)

Leisure and sports
(2.5 hours)

Sleeping
(7.6 hours)

Working and
related activities
(8.8 hours)

Total = 24.0 hours

NOTE: Data include employed persons on days they worked, ages 25 to 54, who lived in households with children under 18. Data include non-holiday weekdays and are annual averages for 2011. Data include related travel for each activity.

SOURCE: Bureau of Labor Statistics, American Time Use Survey

When we are young, we go to work with vim and vigor. Somewhere along the way, we seem to lose that mojo that got us started. We blame it on financial pressures, health issues, family dysfunction, and decide that waiting is a great idea! Waiting for that title, that specific event that will crown us as leaders and take us to success! And while we wait, we blame. We blame the economy, the weather, the bosses, and whatever is handy at any moment. You know that there is a leadership vacuum today – in business, in politics and in our personal lives. What are we going to do about it? As Superman said: *"You've got to look inside; you can't expect some leader to take you anywhere." – Christopher Reeve, 17th April 1997.* That's the essence of "living leadership" daily.

True leaders in everyday life accept leadership as a duty in daily behavior, and begin to break the shackles of this crisis. They practice a set of sustainable daily behaviors that will lead to exceptional performance and, therefore, fulfillment at work.

We learnt in this book that there is a framework of change that you can use. It is called the Leadership Ascent Curve. We focused on specific secrets of great leaders that will drive your leadership behaviors. As we climb the Leadership Ascent Curve:

We will craft our Core. The basic and essential Core of any leader is, first and foremost, competence. Whatever your chosen field is, commit to a relentless pursuit and mastery of those core skills. An incompetent leader is a pretender, at best.

We will focus on accomplishing initiatives. Your competence and core skills need to drive you to *finish* projects. This is key – the starting and finishing of purposeful work, where you are able to use and polish your core skills. Whether you are starting off, changing careers, adding skills, or taking on more responsibility, this is a key building block to the foundation of your platform.

We will "do" credibility. What does this mean? It means that our focus needs to be on "doing" something rather than on "being" someone! We live in the era of the "celebrity" leader. It seems that to show leadership, you have to "be" somebody. It is actually the other way around! You show leadership first, and you become somebody automatically after that. You are credible based on what you accomplish – whether it is a set of outcomes you generate or a set of outcomes you enable in others. Credibility is a result – not an action. It appears, as if magic, once you actively pursue the first two building blocks.

We will work on nurturing and transforming. As Tom Peters famously said, *"Leaders don't create followers, they create leaders."* You now collaborate, connect, and engage yourself and others to a higher level of performance. This is the zone where you can launch not only yourself, but others as well. And you begin to see and understand that the leadership **behavior within yourself** is now actually resulting in **outcomes for others** – the others whom you lead and who have chosen to follow you.

To climb the leadership ascent curve, and to do it the right way – you have to lead by being Humble, Exceptional, Authentic and Transparent. This is the overall umbrella that you have to model your leadership behaviors on. I remember a past client who said that on his way up his own ascent curve, he had made so many enemies, he had destroyed so many relationships that he wondered if there was a better way. I believe that behaving with H.E.A.T. – that is, by being humble, exceptional, authentic and transparent, is a better way.

I want you to get rid of the notion that "leadership is not for everyone" – it is for everyone, especially you!

I also firmly believe that leadership has to start from inside, that is, from within ourselves, and the way we show it, use it, achieve benefits out of it – is through others. We can't serve others if we don't lead from within.

I will leave you with this leadership manifesto:

Our Leadership Way of Life:

We will strive to lead ourselves and others without regard to position or status and find fulfillment: (a) by embracing the duty of leadership as a daily behavior, (b) by a sharp focus on core competence, and (c) by an unflinching intensity on serving and fulfilling others, thereby achieving our purpose.

Our Leadership Resolve:

- We will focus on our core skills and values with a "mad" intensity.

- We will always be partial to positive forward movement.

- We will lead with H.E.A.T – by being **H**umble, **E**xceptional, **A**uthentic & **T**ransparent.

- We will focus on execution and value the outcome and not the credit.

- We will focus on clasping hands rather than wringing hands.

- Every day we will BET on ourselves – **B**e **E**xceptional **T**oday!

ABOUT THE AUTHOR

Vinay Nadig developed the principles and systems around Leadership Escape Velocity – a set of daily leadership behaviors during his 20+ years as a consultant, entrepreneur and a business unit head. Vinay started in the manufacturing sector and as a process and sales engineer he built a solid foundation of systems thinking. Adding an MBA from Texas A&M to his qualifications, Vinay has since concentrated on the systems and processes that "get things done." Along the way, he has consulted with several large Fortune 500 organizations in the healthcare, retail, technology and airline sectors and delivered multi-million dollar initiatives. He has also worked for mid-size global consulting organizations, helping them launch strategic business units.

In all of his experience, Vinay has focused on the set of behaviors within oneself – that can actually result in enabling others to succeed – a system that he lays out in great detail in this book.

Vinay emigrated from India to the USA, on Jan 1st 1990. He holds a Bachelor's Degree in Mechanical Engineering from the University of Mysore, India and an MBA from Texas A & M University, Texas, USA. Vinay lives with his wife and two children in the Dallas, TX area.

Social Media:

- Vinay blogs regularly at http://www.leadershipd-harma.com. Blog entries revolve around the concepts and frameworks that I present in this book.

- Vinay podcasts ("Living Leadership Daily - Leadership Behaviors for Exceptional Performance with Vinay Nadig") and the podcasts are available on iTunes, free of charge.

- Vinay videocasts on youtube. Catch him on his channel at - http://www.youtube.com/user/vinaynadig123/videos

- Vinay tweets regularly @vinaynadig